SPITFIRE

Jeffrey L. Ethell and Steve Pace

Motorbooks International
Publishers & Wholesalers ®

DEDICATION

In memory of Jeffrey L. Ethell, 1947–1997

First published in 1997 by Motorbooks International Publishers & Wholesalers, 729 Prospect Avenue, PO Box 1, Osceola, WI 54020-0001

© Steve Pace, 1997

Edited by: Mike Haenggi
Designed by: Amy T. Huberty

Printed in The United States of America

Library of Congress Cataloging-in-Publication Data Available
ISBN 0-7603-0300-2

On the front cover: After service as an LF.IXE, TE308 was converted to a two-seat Tr.9 for the Irish Air Corps in 1951, then became an instructional airframe. Sold to take part in the *Battle of Britain* film, the aircraft later passed on to Don Plumb in Canada in 1970, who converted to a single seater by covering the rear cockpit. It went to the Owls Head Transportation Museum in Maine in 1975, was sold to Woodson K. Woods of Arizona in 1979, converted back to a two-seater, and finally sold to current owner William S. Greenwood of Aspen, Colorado, in 1983. *Christopher P. Davis*

On the back cover, top: The prototype Griffon-engined Spitfire was DP845, initially rebuilt from a production Merlin-powered airframe and designated the F.IV. Later it became the F.XII, fitted with the Griffon IIB, then the IV and finally the VI. Delays on availability of the Griffon doomed the Mk.IV as a production variant, but when the engine's bugs were worked out, the Mk. XII began to roll off the assembly line in late 1942.-*NASM*

On the back cover, bottom: Mechanics pull the Rolls-Royce Merlin from a 336th Squadron, 4th Fighter Group Mk. V at Audley End, England, in April 1943, just as the group was transitioning to P-47 Thunderbolts. Made up of former Eagle Squadron personnel, the 4th was sad to see its Spitfires go in favor of the massive Republic fighter, but the war was taking them deeper into enemy territory than the Spitfire could go. *USAF*

CONTENTS

ACKNOWLEDGMENTS

This book could not have been produced without the help of these individuals: Dr. Alfred Price; Tom Miller, TranSlides; Robert F. Dorr; Air Vice Marshal Johnnie Johnson (RAF, Ret.); Group Captain David Green (RAF, Ret.), the Spitfire Society; Pilot Officer Tony Ross (RAF); Flight Lieutenant Don Healey (RAF); Flight Lieutenant Charlie Allen (RAF); Squadron Leader Billy Benn (RAF, Ret.); Peter Alexander (RN); Michael Spenser (RAF); John and Pam Dibbs, Flying Legends; Colonel Al Cole (USAF, Ret.); Mike Haenggi; and the editorial staff at Motorbooks International Publishers & Wholesalers. Special thanks to Scott Markam and Don Morgan, Graphic Scenes.

Steve Pace

INTRODUCTION

By the year 1933, the world's ever-growing number of airframe and powerplant manufacturers were just beginning to get their respective acts together. Prior to this time, except for a few standout airplanes and aero engines, the pickings had not been too impressive. At this time, remember, man had only been flying powered aircraft for a mere 30 years. Though 30 years seems like a long time, during the 1903–1933 period, the world of aircraft design had pretty much stagnated. But beginning in 1933, particularly in Great Britain, the wings that were to come were already starting to spread. This was especially true at Vickers-Supermarine and Rolls-Royce, for these two aviation giants were about to join forces to create of one of the best airframe and powerplant combinations in aviation history—a fighter plane called the Spitfire, which proved to be the right fighter at the right time.

When it made its first flight more than 60 years ago in its original prototype form, the first of 20,351 Spitfire airplanes was an instant success for its manufacturer. Moreover, with 2,408 navalized versions, called the Seafire, also built, this was indeed a lucrative airplane production program. While it is true that the Spitfire and Seafire aircraft production programs generated large sums of cash, their greatest values were priceless, in that they helped the Royal Air Force (RAF) and the Royal Navy (RN) win World War II, which for the United Kingdom began on 3 September 1939. In fact, most aviation historians agree that without the Spitfire, the Battle of Britain might have been lost to Germany.

By mid-1942, when they were needed most, a new generation of Spitfires were entering service with the Royal Air Force, in an effort to match the Luftwaffe's newest strain of fighters. These later Spitfires, comprising the Mk VI, Mk VIII, Mk IX, Mk XII, Mk XIV, and Mk XVI, featured vast improvements in altitude, range, and firepower. These improvements helped revive the RAF's air superiority, which was declining during the 1943–44 period.

Likewise, with later Seafires, made up of the Mk III, Mk XV, and others, the Royal Navy's contribution to the war increased dramatically, which helped turn the tide of defeat away from England and back toward Germany.

Powered by either the Rolls-Royce Merlin or the Rolls-Royce Griffon series of inline liquid-cooled V-12 engines, spinning two-, three-, four-, five-, and even six-bladed propellers, depending on the application, the many different versions of the Spitfire and Seafire enjoyed continuing increases in performance throughout their lives. While the original Spitfire was clocked at 349.5 miles per hour, the final version was timed at more than 450 miles per hour. Not to be forgotten, their rate of climb escalated from 2,500 feet per minute to more than 4,500 feet per minute, and with their progressively newer and better armament capabilities, their rates of fire grew from 240 to 720 rounds per minute.

During production, from 1936 to 1949, there came 24 Mks or versions of the Spitfire, and 8 of the navalized Seafire. The later versions of these aircraft served as first-line fighters until the mid-1950s, demonstrating their effectiveness as dedicated warbirds well into the jet age.

The Spitfire and the Seafire were employed for numerous operational duties. They served as area- and point-defense interceptors, eye-to-eye air combat dogfighters, armed and unarmed photographic reconnaissance aircraft, and as fighter-bombers.

But in one unique combat scenario that no one had foreseen at the start of the war, they were called upon to pursue and destroy Germany's incoming fleets of pulsejet-powered, pilotless V-1 "buzz bombs," which had rained down upon England. Thanks to the Spitfire and Seafire aircraft and their driven pilots, many of the V-1s were destroyed before they could reach their targets.

Moreover, on 5 October 1944, a Mk XIV of RAF No. 401 Squadron claimed the first Messerschmitt Me 262 turbojet-powered fighter to be shot down by any allied fighter plane. This was the first time in history that a propeller-driven fighter had shot down a jet fighter—a new breed, with a 100-mile per hour speed advantage.

Some seven years after World War II, a photographic reconnaissance Spitfire Mk XIX of No. 81 Squadron flying out of Hong Kong on 5 February 1952, accomplished what seemed to be an impossible feat, when it flew faster and higher than any other piston-powered airplane had ever flown. RAF Flight Lieutenant Ted Powles attained an incredible speed of 690 miles per hour (Mach 0.94, or more than 9/10ths the speed of sound) during an emergency dive that had begun at an unheard of but true altitude of 51,550 feet during a high-altitude test flight. To say the Spitfire and Seafire aircraft were not tough birds would be a major understatement.

Fighting in concert with other exceptional allied fighter planes, such as the British Hurricane and Typhoon and the American Lightning, Mustang, and Thunderbolt, the Spitfires and Seafires played a decisive and dynamic part in the United Kingdom's valiant effort to trash Hitler's war machine and win World War II. They most assuredly are warbirds to be remembered.

DEVELOPMENTAL HIGHLIGHTS

Military leaders often sanction weapons that might have won the previous war. Other men, rarer in mold and enriched with foresight, envision weapons that may be valuable in future confrontations. One such man was U.S. Army Air Service Brigadier General William E. Mitchell (Billy). From the harassing-by-hand bombardment sorties of World War I, Mitchell foresaw immense squadrons of bombardment aircraft destroying all in their path. But, in pleading his case with military planners, he was met with laughter and contempt.

During the period 13–21 July 1921, Mitchell's U.S. Army Air Service Martin MB-2 bombers unloaded a bevy of bombs during a series of U.S. Army- and U.S. Navy-sponsored tests, sinking outdated U.S. warships and captured World War I German warships off the coast of Virginia. Proudly, Mitchell pointed to the sinking hulks and said, "That's what bombers can do!"

Unconvinced and pointing out that the ships were anchored. unarmed and defenseless, the conservative U.S. armed forces hierarchy scorned Mitchell's theories and persisted in their reliance on conventional weapons, especially naval sea power. But Mitchell would not be put aside, and his constant criticism led to his unjust court-martial in 1925. He was stripped of his command and reduced in rank to colonel. Billy Mitchell died at the age of 57 on 19 February 1936, at a time when his beliefs were finally being realized. Correctly, he was posthumously elevated to the higher rank of major general, and today he is regarded as one of the architects of U.S. air power.

Foreign powers were not blind to occurrences across the oceans. Germany demonstrated that fact during the Spanish Civil War of 1936, employing aircraft as an integrated element of their infamous blitzkrieg. This German head-start prompted the British to champion progressive warbirds of their own. And so the legendary Spitfire was born.

Beginning in the year of Billy Mitchell's court-martial, a cool, calm, and collected 30-year-old airplane designer named Reginald J. Mitchell was hard at work on a series of ultrafast seaplanes that were being raced in the famed Schneider Trophy Races. These high-speed race planes culminated in the Supermarine S.6B which, with its average speed of 340.08 miles per hour, won the coveted trophy for England in 1931. Two weeks later, the same racing plane upped the world speed record to 407.5 miles per hour. With his winning series of seaplane designs, Reginald Mitchell had more than proved his worth to Supermarine, and to his country. But like most genius aircraft designers, he was never fully satisfied. This became obvious with the Supermarine Type 224, a prototype fighter for the RAF which, due to fluctuating specifications, would never meet his standard of excellence.

The Supermarine Type 224 was a single-seat, single-engine fighter plane optimized to meet the British Air Ministry F.7/30 specifications. It had an inverted gull-type wing, a 600-horsepower steam-cooled Rolls-Royce Goshawk engine, fixed landing gear, four machine guns, and an open cockpit. It was unofficially named Spitfire, but failed as a viable fighter plane, and development was discontinued. In an unsolicited venture, R. J. Mitchell began work on a new and improved fighter, even before the Type 224 prototype had

When the prototype Spitfire, K5054, emerged from the struggles with the aborted Supermarine Type 224, the family resemblance was almost impossible to see. The fixed-landing-gear, open-cockpit 224 monoplane reached only 228-miles-per-hour maximum speed. It was certainly inelegant compared to the slim Spitfire, which flew for the first time on 5 March 1936, at the hands of Vickers-Supermarine chief test pilot Joseph Summers (Mutt). Here K5054 warms up for a test flight on 16 June 1936, just three months into its test program. *Alfred Price*

first taken wing. In doing so, he came up with a similar, but much sleeker, design with an enclosed cockpit and retractable landing gear. This revised Type 300 design drew new interest from the British Air Ministry. After its evaluation, the ministry issued specification F.5/34 for the plane. But this time it was to have eight, not four, machine guns, and it was to be powered by what was to become the famed Rolls-Royce Merlin engine, known then as the PV-12, a liquid-cooled V-type engine rated at 990 takeoff horsepower at sea level.

In creating the Vickers-Supermarine Type 300 prototype, Mitchell had moved well past his original F.5/30 design. The result: The British Air Ministry awarded Supermarine a contract in January 1935 for a single fighter prototype under specification F.37/34, to be ready for flight in one year.

The last full-scale mockup inspection was finalized at Vickers-Supermarine's Woolston facility just three months later. And in less than a year, the prototype, to be officially named Spitfire in June 1936, was prepared for flight.

With Vickers-Supermarine chief test pilot Joseph Summers (Mutt) at the controls on 5

March 1936, the premier Type 300 lifted off from Eastleigh airfield at Southampton. Powered by its Rolls-Royce Merlin Type C engine, it made a successful and near perfect first flight. (Author's note: Vickers in 1928 had obtained all shares of stock of the Supermarine Company, and when the Type 300 prototype flew, Supermarine was the aircraft manufacturing division of Vickers; thus, Vickers-Supermarine.)

There had been clear skies on 5 March, with moderate to good visibility and light southwesterly winds. The flight lasted some 20 minutes, during which the landing gear remained extended and locked, and a simulated landing was made at an altitude of 5,000 feet. Following his initial test hop, while still in his seat, Summers was reported to have said: "I don't want anything touched." He did not have any serious squawks and had found the plane's flying qualities to be quite satisfactory. Apparently the prototype Type 300 was very close to a thing of perfection. R. J. Mitchell was pleased.

To create the Type 300 prototype, Mitchell opted to design its wing using a high-speed

R. J. Mitchell's master work, the prototype Spitfire, is readied for a test flight at Supermarine Aviation Works, a division of Vickers Aviation, in May 1936, when it still had landing-gear door flap fairings, no radio mast, and no guns. The Rolls-Royce 990-horsepower PV.12 engine (later known as the Merlin) was the last step in making Mitchell's dream of a world-beating, thin-winged fighter come true. *Alfred Price*

U.S. National Advisory Committee for Aeronautics (NACA; now National Aeronautics and Space Administration, or NASA) Number 2200 airfoil section of a near-perfect elliptical planform. He designed the tail surfaces to be elliptical as well. And except for the wing flaps, ailerons, rudder, and elevators being covered in fabric, the rest of the airframe was of stressed-skin, all-metal construction.

The Type 300's fuselage comprised three modules: the forward section, housing the Rolls-Royce Merlin engine, firewall, and two fuel tanks, one above the other; the center section, encompassing the cockpit, wing carry-through member, electrical wiring, fuel lines, and hydraulic fluid lines; and the aft section, supporting the tail surfaces. While the forward module was of tubular construction, the center and aft modules of the fuselage were of monocoque fabrication.

The thin-section elliptical wings were designed to house eight Browning .303-caliber machine guns. And except for the wing leading edge, it was too thin and too crowded with guns

and ammunition to hold fuel tanks (though later versions had leading-edge wing tanks).

When it first appeared, the Vickers Type 300 prototype was a unique, sleek, and aerodynamically beautiful fighter-type airplane. Mitchell had molded an eye-catching design around a very large 12-cylinder V-type engine and a somewhat small but adequate cockpit. Ammunition boxes for its eight machine guns could hold 300 rounds each.

The Type 300's powerplant was the soon-to-become-immortal Rolls-Royce Merlin, a V-type housing 12 cylinders—six in either bank, which were outwardly angled at 60 degrees. The Merlin was cooled exclusively by ethylene glycol, which did not boil; it had originally been engineered to be cooled by water which did boil. Later Merlin engines were water-cooled, but with a 30-percent mixture of ethylene glycol antifreeze. It was found that at temperatures of up to 275 degrees Fahrenheit, with the 30-percent ethylene glycol, the engines would not boil over.

Each of the Merlin V-12's cylinders had a piston bore size of 5.4 inches and a connecting rod stroke of 6 inches, which gave it a 1,649-cubic-inch displacement, though they were most commonly referred to as 1,650-cid engines. The original Merlin engine and its later versions employed dual tandem gear-driven two-stage supercharging units, which substantially increased horsepower without the addition of too much weight.

As it turned out, the Rolls-Royce Merlin series of powerplants became the single most important British designed and built engines of World War II. The Merlin's maximum takeoff horsepower ratings grew from 990 to more than 1,720 horsepower during its development cycle. It became a landmark engine series in the truest sense of that word, and the Merlin Type C engine of 990 horsepower, coupled with the Vickers-Supermarine Type 300 prototype's airframe, spelled immediate success for Mitchell's greatest aircraft design.

• • •

Type 300 Prototype Specifications

Wing span	37 feet, 0 inches
Length	29 feet, 11 inches
Height	12 feet, 8 inches
Powerplant	990-horsepower Rolls-Royce Merlin Type C; 1,045-horsepower Rolls-Royce Merlin Type F after 1 January 1937
Armament	Eight Browning .303 machine guns after being brought up to Mk I production standard; 300 rounds per gun (2,400 total rounds)
Maximum speed	380 miles per hour indicated at maximum limiting speed
Maximum range	350–400 miles (best estimate; not established)
Rate of climb	2,400 feet per minute at sea level
Service ceiling	35,400 feet

• • •

Vickers-Supermarine Chairman Sir Robert McLean had felt deeply in 1935 that the Type 300 prototype should have an official name. He let it be known that the plane's name should begin with the letter "S" for Supermarine, and that the name should sound poisonous in nature.

The first production Spitfire Mk I, K9787, on the ramp at Martlesham Heath for service testing, first flew on 14 May 1938. The aircraft's real lineage, the Schneider Cup racers, was more than evident in the fighter's clean lines. Mitchell died before seeing a single production Spitfire fly, and design work was taken over by his assistant, Joe Smith. The aircraft was acknowledged as elegant by any standard, clearly designed by an aircraft enthusiast who was much more than a slide-rule user. *Alfred Price*

Numerous monikers popped up, such as Serpent, Venom, and Viper, as did Spitfire, which had been used earlier on an unofficial basis for the Type 224. Neither the British Air Ministry nor R. J. Mitchell approved of the latter name. Still, the flock of names for the Type 300 were submitted to the British Air Ministry for its selection processes with a note from McLean suggesting that the name Spitfire sounded best after the Supermarine. But being his design, and not wanting it to be named Spitfire, Mitchell was later heard to describe the McLean-suggested name as "bloody silly." Yet on 10 June 1936, just three months after the Type 300 prototype had first taken wing, the British Air Ministry approved the name that Mitchell had thought to be inappropriate. And with that, what was to become the deadly Spitfire, which proved itself to be a potent adversary indeed, was born. With up to 12 engine exhaust pipes and as many as eight gun barrels all spitting fire simultaneously, the name proved quite appropriate.

Soon after the Type 300's first flight, with its original two-bladed, fine-pitched wooden propeller having been replaced by a normal-pitch type, Vickers-Supermarine test pilots Mutt Summers, Jeffrey Quill, and George Pickering continued to wring her out over the south of England. And on 26 March 1936, George Pickering deliv-

The seventh production Mark I, K9793, here at Martlesham Heath in July 1939, was fitted with a Merlin II engine and a two-position de Havilland metal propeller, yielding a great improvement in takeoff performance and an extra 4 miles per hour in top speed. From the 78th production aircraft on, this prop was made standard. Eight Browning .303 machine guns were fitted as regulation armament. The initial flat cockpit canopy is clearly evident on the aircraft . . . a bulged bubble was fitted as normal before the war began. *Alfred Price*

ered her (Royal Air Force Serial Number K5054) to Martlesham Heath for all-out performance tests. The ensuing high-speed trials showed the infant fighter plane could produce a very mature top speed of 430 miles per hour in a shallow dive, a fantastic speed that later versions would surpass in level-attitude flight!

The performance trials culminated in mid-June, and on 18 June, it was returned to Eastleigh, where it was first displayed publicly, to about 300 invited aircraft community guests. During its unveiling ceremonies that day, both on the ground and in the air, the Spitfire showed its character. When an oil line broke during one of the demonstrations, and pilot Jeffrey Quill was still able to land without incident, it further impressed the audience.

It was a good airplane, and at the Hendon Air Pageant on 27 June, while being flown by Royal Air Force (RAF) Flight Lieutenant J. H. Edwards-Jones, it was shown to all in attendance. Three days later, at the Society of British Aircraft Con-

structors' convention at Hatfield, Mutt Summers put K5054 through its paces, earning even more respect and proving that the Spitfire was for real.

Following its subsequent spin trials at Farnborough, and after its return to Eastleigh for a few modifications and additional test hops, K5054 was ferried back to Martlesham Heath on 23 February 1937 to undergo complete handling characteristics trials. When these trials had been completed, Vickers-Supermarine was able to boast of a 330-mile-per-hour true air speed in level flight at an altitude of 10,000 feet, 349.5 miles per hour at 16,800 feet, and 324 miles per hour at 30,000 feet. And with its 1,770-feet-per-minute rate of climb it could level off at 20,000 feet after only 8 minutes and 12 seconds; but at sea level, its rate of climb was raised to 2,400 feet per minute. In total, Mitchell's masterpiece had surpassed the British Air Ministry's original performance demands by a large margin.

Following additional modifications, such as the installation of the more powerful 1,045-

The calm before the storm in the summer of 1939 . . . a beautiful echelon of No. 65 Squadron Mk Is form up over the clouds. All are fitted with three-bladed propellers and bulged canopies. The Spitfire was also modified in ways less visible, with a bullet-proof windscreen, armor plate for the firewall and the pilot, and an engine-driven hydraulic pump for the landing gear. In early Mk Is, the pilot had to get the gear up with a hand pump. *Alfred Price*

horsepower Merlin Type F engine, a reflector-type gun sight, better aileron controls, and a rotating tailwheel in place of the original fixed skid-type unit, Spitfire Number One continued in its quest for immortality. But on 22 March 1937, it suffered a minor setback.

As it happened that day, while it was being flown by RAF Flight Lieutenant J. F. McKenna at Eastleigh, the new Type F Merlin engine lost oil pressure. The friction subsequently became too great within the engine, and it began running too rough for continued operation. McKenna wisely shut everything down to make a good but scary dead stick, wheels-up belly landing. Luckily, the damage to K5054 was light, and after minor repairs, it was again in the air.

After his four-year battle with cancer, Reginald J. Mitchell died on 11 June 1937, at the age of 42.

For more than a year, he watched as his beloved Type 300 prototype grew out of its infancy, entered puberty, and earned the right to be reproduced. Though he never saw another Spitfire fly other than his Number One, he was well aware of its future potential, knowing the British Air Ministry had ordered 310 additional examples over a year earlier, on 3 June 1936 (the second largest initial aircraft order in British history).

As chief designer at Vickers-Supermarine, Mitchell was replaced by Joseph Smith, who ultimately became responsible for all further designs and developments on every subsequent Spitfire type to come about during the next 10 or so years. As it turned out, Smith, prior assistant to Mitchell, did a great service to his former boss and country.

Armed, Deadly, and Ready to Fight

One important factor in the lives of the RAF's Spitfire and the Royal Navy's follow-on Seafire aircraft was their armament capabilities. Ultimately, as with any dedicated warbirds, their armaments were wide-ranging; that is, they carried everything from machine guns, to cannons, to bombs, to rockets. But not at first. In fact, as had been planned originally, early production Type 300 aircraft were to be armed with four instead of eight wing-mounted .303 machine guns. Yet even before Spitfire Number One flew, it had been decided to arm production aircraft with eight machine guns, as four .303 guns gave too little firepower. But at first, these machine guns were not in adequate supply, and only four per airplane could be installed.

In May 1938, after it had received its required armament of eight .303 Browning machine guns, the premier Spitfire began armament trials at Martlesham Heath, using the newly developed Type GD 5 reflector-type gun sight by Barr and Stroud, and a Type G 22 gun camera. By now, it had been upgraded to production Mk I Spitfire standard, which included the RAF camouflage paint job. Early gun heating and jamming problems arose, but when they were corrected, the firing trials became successful. More important, toward the conclusion of the extensive gun evaluation flights, it was realized that the Spitfire's concentrated firepower from eight guns was not only accurate but exceedingly destructive to a target.

Full-scale production was ordered 3 June 1936 with the original 310-plane order, and new Spitfire Mk I fighters slowly began to roll off their assembly lines by mid-1938.

On 15 May 1938 at Eastleigh, with Jeffrey Quill in control, the first production Spitfire Mk I (K9787) made a successful first flight. Powered by the Mk II version of the Merlin engine, which had a crankshaft speed of 3,000 revolutions per minute, and produced 1,030 horsepower, this first production version of the Spitfire hit 470 miles per hour in a dive test; its best level flight speed was 362 miles per hour at an altitude of 18,500 feet. It featured a service ceiling of 31,900 feet (service ceiling in this case is where the rate of climb was no more than 100 feet per minute). And with its 2,065-feet-per-minute rate of climb at sea level, it could reach a height of 15,000 feet in six minutes and 30 seconds.

Spitfire Mk I deliveries were more than slow at the start of production, largely due to Vickers-Supermarine's limited facilities. Gearing up for such a large order (only the order for 600 Hawker Hurricane fighters had been larger) was troublesome, and Vickers, the parent company of Supermarine, came up with a viable and relatively new solution: subcontracting, or what would be known in later decades as "outsourcing." In other words, other contractors would supply Spitfire components. Initial production was slow, and only a mere 49 Spitfires had been delivered by the beginning of the year 1939.

On 19 July 1938, the second production Spitfire Mk I (K9788) was delivered to the RAF at Martlesham Heath, where it too would be thoroughly evaluated.

It had been decided that the No. 12 Group, No. 19 Squadron of RAF Fighter Command at Duxford, England, would be the first unit to receive production Spitfires. And on 4 August 1938, it got its first Spitfire Mk I (K9789), the third one produced.

Earlier, to better distinguish production Spitfires from the one-of-a-kind prototype, the British Air Ministry issued specification F.16/36, which included a number of minor changes. These included stiffening the wings to allow 450-miles-per-hour air speed without flutter; increased fuel capacity (from 85 to 94 gallons); use of a fixed-pitch two-bladed Airscrew Company wooden propeller with a diameter of 10 feet, 8 inches; and increased flap travel (from 57 to 85 degrees). Production moved forward, and by mid-1939 serious war clouds were gathering everywhere over Europe , as Germany was boldly demonstrating its aggressiveness almost daily.

Then on 1 September 1939, Germany invaded Poland. Great Britain and France immediately gave Hitler their ultimatums to pull back, which he, of course, ignored. Two days later, in their combined efforts to halt his aggression before it was too late, both nations declared war on Germany. But Hitler's healthy war machine was on the move, and at the time, it did appear that it was already too late.

The day after England declared war on Germany, the one-off Spitfire Type 300 prototype suffered a fatal crash, after a 45-minute test hop out of Farnborough. At about 3:15 P.M. on 4 September 1939, with RAF Flight Lieutenant G. S. White (Spinner) under glass, the first-ever Spitfire crash-landed and flipped onto its back. White died later from his injuries, and the plane itself was damaged beyond repair. The original Spitfire was gone, but its legacy was sure to live on.

By this time a total of nine RAF fighter

It wasn't long before RAF planners looked at the fast, nimble Spitfire as an ideal photo reconnaissance platform. This PR.IC, near Heston in 1941 with Flying Officer S. Wise in the cockpit, has the one-piece windscreen that was fitted to most recce versions. The first photo mission by a converted Mk I Spitfire was made in November 1939 in France. The advantages of the new installation were immediately obvious, the primary being the ability to avoid enemy fighters with high speed. *Alfred Price*

squadrons had been fully equipped with new Spitfire Mk I airplanes. Two additional RAF squadrons, 603 and 609, were just beginning to get their Mk Is. And, of course, many more would follow.

Germany's Luftwaffe Over England

Two RAF fighter squadrons, 602 and 603, which were Auxiliary Air Force Squadrons of Scotland, became the first Spitfire units to make contact with Germany's Luftwaffe (air force) over England. Operating out of Drem and Turnhouse on 16 October 1939, Nos. 602 and 603 Squadrons encountered a number of Junkers Ju 88s that were attacking British warships at the Firth of Forth in the North Sea, especially targeting the famed HMS *Hood*. And without any combat experience, these Scottish fighter pilots were able to down at least five of the Ju 88s they had come up against.

Throughout the remainder of 1939 and into the beginning of 1940, Spitfire production was stepped up dramatically. Still, on 10 May 1940, when Germany invaded France, there were not enough Spitfires there to do much good against the numerous Luftwaffe aircraft. England, knowing full well that it was high (if not on the top) of Hitler's wish list of the countries he wanted to conquer, fought valiantly with what arms and armor it had. In the meantime, Vickers-Supermarine continued to improve upon and manufacture its needed Spitfire fighters.

With the requirement of much more firepower than could be brought to bear with its eight small-bore .303 inch machine guns, the "B" version of the Mk I was developed. The Mk IB featured a special wing, logically dubbed the B wing, to house four .303 machine guns and two Hispano 20-mm cannons. This was the first version of the Spitfire to be considered a deadly weapon against the Axis powers.

As good as Germany's combat aircraft and pilots were at the time, the relatively new fleet of Spitfires and their apprentice combat pilots had also begun to pass the test. Having earned their spurs in combat, both entities appeared to be ready for any and all forthcoming aggression. By mid-1940, when it became obvious that Germany would soon increase its attacks on England, a serious question arose about the availability of front-line fighters: Was there too little too late?

During the mid-1937 to mid-1940 period, even though the British Air Ministry had put forth its firm requirement for up to 2,000 advanced fighter aircraft, such as the Hawker Hurricane and Vickers-Supermarine Spitfire, fewer than 800 existed when they were to face the next test: The Battle of Britain.

THE BATTLE OF BRITAIN

For the English, the relatively short Battle of Britain seemed to last forever. According to the RAF, the Battle of Britain officially began 8 August 1940 and ended 31 October 1940. If not for the limited availability of the Hurricanes and Spit-fires, the RAF might not have been able to hold off Hitler's Luftwaffe. Most fortunately, when the Battle of Britain commenced, the RAF had 19 Spitfire-equipped fighter squadrons ready for combat.

The Spitfire Mk I was the single version of the aircraft to fight during the Battle of Britain. Retaining the clean lines of the prototype, the Mk I had about the same performance as its arch rival, the Messerschmitt 109E, and could get to altitude faster than its stable mate, the Hurricane, which was usually assigned to attack the Luftwaffe bomber streams. *USAF*

The two main fighter antagonists of the Battle of Britain go at it in the skies over England . . . almost. Actually this is a staged German propaganda photo, which originally appeared in color, of a captured Spitfire with bogus markings being "chased" by an Me 109E over the continent. If a Spitfire Mk I pilot were really in this predicament, he would not be able to nose over, as the carburetor float would cut the fuel flow to the engine . . . a genuine operational liability. *Alfred Price*

First blood had been drawn earlier, however, when a 603 Squadron Spitfire Mk I downed a Heinkel He 111 on 16 October 1939, the first German airplane destroyed over English territory in World War II, and the first downed by a British fighter since World War I.

When the Battle of Britain began, the RAF's two best fighters, Hurricanes and Spitfires, were not as plentiful as the RAF would have liked. Because at the time there were only about 650 of both types available, with a ratio of about two Spitfires to three Hurricanes. Amazingly, that incredibly small number of front-line fighters were able to repel the German Luftwaffe.

The reason more Hurricanes were available was that the RAF, through the British Air Ministry, had ordered them first and in larger numbers. It had ordered 600 Hurricane Mk Is on 3 June 1936, some six months after the Hurricane prototype (K5083) had made its first flight on 6 November 1935, more than four months before

the Spitfire was first flown. One month after Hawker received its 600-plane order, on 3 July 1936, Vickers-Supermarine got its initial production order for 310 Spitfire Mk Is.

When the Battle of Britain got underway only 396 Hurricanes and 228 Spitfires were available to fly and fight. During the battle, Hurricanes are credited with downing 627 enemy aircraft, compared with the Spitfire's total of 521.5. Today, of course, each type's kill rate is what really matters. According to RAF Group Captain David J. Green, founder and chairman of the Spitfire Society, these all-important kill rates "may be judged from the fact that the Hurricanes fielded 33 squadrons, compared to the Spitfire's 19 units."

The battle actually traces back to 16 July 1940, when Adolf Hitler signed German War Directive No. 16, for *Seelöwe* or Operation Sea Lion. The operation against England was to begin with a vast aerial assault by the Luftwaffe, and was to be intensified with naval and ground (para-

Although the Messerschmitt 109 remained the contemporary of the Spitfire throughout World War II, their classic confrontation was during the Battle of Britain. "White 10," a *1.Staffel, Jagdgeschwader 26* Me 109E-4, taxies out from its base in France for a mission over England in that fateful summer of 1940. The yellow nose became a trademark for JG 26, eventually leading to their nickname among Allied crews as the "Yellow-Nosed Abbeville Kids."

trooper) activities after 1 August 1940. The first paragraph of his follow-on Directive No. 17 read: "Using all possible means, the German air forces will smash the British air forces in as brief a period of time as possible. Its attacks will be directed in the first instance against formations in flight, their ground facilities, and their supply centers, then against the British aircraft industry, including factories producing anti-aircraft guns."

In the first aerial battles, RAF Spitfire pilots accounted well for themselves. The RAF Hawker Hurricanes in greater numbers fought hard as well, but it was the Spitfires that more quickly gained fame.

A British Air Ministry booklet on the Battle of Britain points out four distinct phases: (1.) From 8 to 18 August, Germany launched an all-out attack on English Channel warship convoys, the southeastern coastline and harbors of England and the military air bases in those areas; (2.) From 19 August to 5 September, the Luftwaffe was directed to destroy inland fighter air bases; (3.) From 6 September to 5 October, Germany launched full-scale aerial attacks on London; (4.) From 6 to 31 Octo-

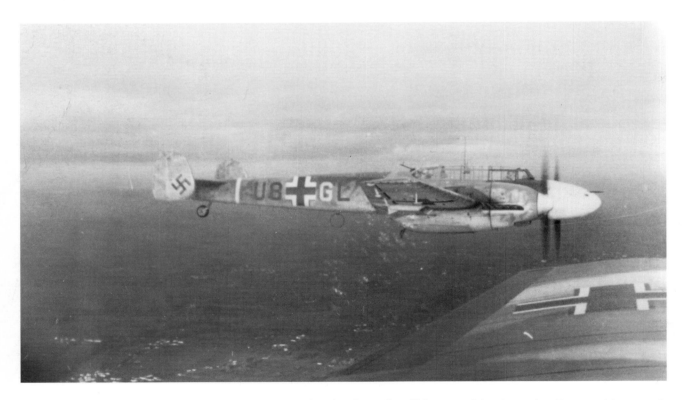

Though the Messerschmitt 110 was supposed to be the Luftwaffe's powerful twin-engine *Zerstörer* (destroyer) fighter, it ended up as easy meat for the Spitfire and the Hurricane. A 3.Staffel, ZG 26 Me 110C cruises across France toward England in 1940, just off the wing of its Rotte leader. When the aircraft's formidable forward firing armament could be brought to bear, it was quite deadly.

ber, and actually continuing thereafter, the Luftwaffe attacked the whole of Britain during nighttime raids against all vital targets.

During the period 10 July to 31 October 1940, Germany lost a total of 1,733 aircraft of all types, compared to England's loss of 915 aircraft and 415 pilots.

To actually accomplish that feat, England was able to unleash just 396 Hurricanes and 228 Spitfires, or a total of 624 front-line fighters. In July 1940, the RAF had 1,341 trained pilots, bolstered by pilots of Coastal Command and the Royal Navy Fleet Air Arm, as well as one hastily formed Czech squadron and four Polish squadrons.

From the other side of the English Channel, Luftwaffe Commander in Chief Hermann Göring sent a total of 1,733 German fighter planes into battle. For the most part, these included the single-engine Messerschmitt Me 109 and the twin-engined Messerschmitt Me

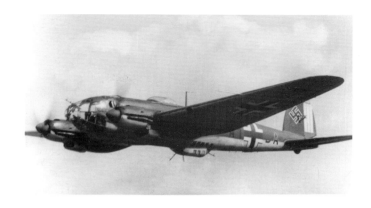

The main Luftwaffe bomber of the Battle of Britain, the Heinkel 111, remained a major target for RAF Fighter Command's fighters. This *Kampfgeschwader 53/Stab* He 111H-2 climbs toward England from its French base in the summer of 1940. While Spitfires held off the 109 fighter cover, Hurricanes went after the bombers.

The Luftwaffe's finest Battle of Britain bomber was the Junkers 88, designed from the start as a Snellbomber, or fast bomber. These *Schwartzmänner*, or ground crew, push the tail of a 3./KG 51 *Edelweiss* Ju 88A-1 around on the unit's ramp in France during the summer of 1940, prior to a mission over England. With bombs gone and power up, the Junkers was a challenge to catch, even in a Spitfire.

The third Luftwaffe bomber used in the Battle of Britain was the Dornier 17Z, an underpowered version of the earlier Do 17, nicknamed "the flying pencil," due to its slim fuselage. Concentrating the crew in the nose required a redesign, which bulged the nose on the Z and slowed it down, making it a target for skilled British fighter pilots. Here a *Stab/KG 3* Do 17Z is readied for a mission from France in the summer of 1940.

110. While the former was a more than adequate foe, the latter was little threat to the fighters of Great Britain. Yet, during the two months and 23 days of the conflict, England's air forces lost a total of 915 aircraft of all types for an amazing differential of 818 airplanes.

Also greatly helping England's cause was its newly established, yet extremely thorough, network of radar installations called, "Chain Home." This primitive early warning system gave the RAF Fighter Command barely enough time to get its aircraft airborne and on track to meet the Me 109s, Me 110s, and others. This radar network extended from the Shetland Islands (north of Scotland) to Land's End, at the western extremity of the English Channel. Göring quickly realized the strategic significance of Britain's radar stations and immediately ordered them attacked.

These attacks on England's radar and on the forward fighter bases network from 8 to 15 August 1940 came mostly from Scandinavian bases. They were fierce and costly to the RAF, but for some unknown reason, Göring put a halt to

Scramble! This No. 313 (Czech) Squadron pilot is just about to leap into his Mark I, engine running, and warm thanks to the somewhat nonchalant ground crewman on the wing waiting to strap him in. The RAF, and the Luftwaffe on the other side of the Channel, brought scrambling to a fine art during the Battle of Britain. Pilots were able to get into the air from sitting in a chair in a matter of minutes. *Alfred Price*

A No. 19 Squadron Spitfire I is quickly rearmed during the Battle of Britain. The sergeant pilot waits in the cockpit; if he's lucky, his ground crew will have given him something to drink or eat in the few minutes he is on the ground. Rearming a Spitfire was not a major task, thanks to the bottom wing panels opening up. *Alfred Price*

these attacks, which spared England from numerous other surprise aerial attacks and possible devastation. Going back to 8 August then, Britain lost 303 to Germany's 403 aircraft of all types. Going further back to 10 July, these totals were 472 to 595 aircraft of all types, respectively.

With England's radar network up and running, it easily detected incoming enemy aircraft during the remaining phases of the Battle of Britain. From 24 August to 6 September, for example, the Luftwaffe sent over numerous Me 110 fighter-bombers and Junkers Ju 87 dive bombers to attack aircraft production factories and inland fighter bases. Escorted by Me 109 fighters, the Me 110s and Ju 87s suffered heavy losses, thanks to the many Me 109s destroyed primarily by the RAF Hurricanes and Spitfires. In the final outcome of this phase, Britain lost 262 to Germany's 378 aircraft of all types.

In one particular phase from 7 to 15 September—1 to 31 October 1940, RAF Fighter Command

ber 1940, all hell freed itself, as Germany put forth an all-out effort to destroy London and all of the remaining British aircraft. In this phase, Britain lost 380 to Germany's 435 aircraft of all types. This defeat caused Germany to postpone indefinitely , and actually cancel, Operation Sea Lion, and to initiate high-altitude bombardment raids. These, for the most part, proved to be insufficient. On 15 September alone, RAF Fighter Command shot down some 70 German bombers and fighters, while it lost only 28 Hurricanes and Spitfires. This victory was a much needed morale booster for the English people on the whole, and for the RAF in particular. Furthermore, it pretty much announced to Germany that it had better rethink its war strategy and revise its aerial tactics. This fact became very obvious in the final phase of the battle.

In the last phase of the Battle of Britain—1 to 31 October 1940, RAF Fighter Command

The Battle of Britain was also fought by the Spitfire Photo Development Unit (Reconnaissance Unit, as of July 1940), so new it didn't even have a number assigned to it. The underwing bulges on this PR.IF were 30-gallon fuel tanks. With another 29 gallons behind the cockpit, the aircraft carried more than double the fuel in the Mk I fighter. Two cameras were carried in the rear fuselage. *Alfred Price*

enjoyed the arrivals of ever-increasing numbers of Hurricanes, Spitfires, and freshly trained pilots to man them. Germany, in preparation for its final assault, covered England's southern and eastern territories with inadequate fighter-bomber sweeps that were easily repelled. And when Halloween arrived in 1940, it had become abundantly clear to Germany that England was in no mood whatsoever to give away any treats. Instead, the German people had finally realized that Hitler had tricked them into believing that the numerous attacks on England would be easy. Obviously, by listening to their leader, the Germans had forgotten the determination of the British people, proven in World War I.

While it remains true that the Battle of Britain officially lasted from 8 August to 31 October 1940, few Britons will agree with those dates. In their minds, it really ran from 3 September 1939 to 2 September 1945. For England, however, that particular battle became a turning point toward the outcome of the war some five years later.

Prime Minister Winston Churchill, who had taken over on 10 May 1940 after the resignation of Neville Chamberlain, said it best: "Never in the field of human conflict was so much owed by so many to so few."

It was not only the Spitfires and their brave pilots that had turned back Hitler's deadly war machine during the Battle of Britain, but both had met the challenge. As a result, these famed fighter planes and their dedicated pilots would forever be known as members of "the few."

A Spitfire PR.IC with the Photographic Reconnaissance Unit is readied for a sortie over France during the Battle of Britain. Photo-recce flying was more than dangerous with unarmed aircraft, but the pictures showing enemy strength and installations were considered critical. *Alfred Price*

The PRU Spitfires, including this PR.IC at Heston, roamed the continent during the summer of 1940. Missions were flown at the highest possible altitudes or very low levels to avoid both flak and interceptors. Though PRU Spitfire pilots got virtually none of the publicity accorded their fighter brethren, they pioneered the fine art of laying the enemy bare in the face of daunting odds. *R. C. Jones via Alfred Price*

COMBAT ACTION

Starting with England's and France's declaration of war with Germany on 3 September 1939 and finishing with V-J Day on 2 September 1945, the Vickers-Supermarine Spitfire series of warplanes earned the distinction of being the longest-battling fighter type of all the Allied combat aircraft in World War II. Spitfires spread their elliptical wings over most of the world, fighting in Europe, the Middle and Far East, the Middle and South Pacific, and the North Atlantic.

It was some 10 months before the Battle of Britain that Germany's Luftwaffe aircraft first entered into the skies over Great Britain. This happened initially on 16 October 1939, when Heinkel

As the winter of 1940–41 set in, fighter operations on both sides ground down to a near halt in the face of atrocious weather. The Spitfire was primarily a day, clear-air interceptor, so it often sat under wraps in the ice and snow waiting for the renewal of operations in the spring. *USAF*

He 111 bombers and Junkers Ju 88 dive bombers flew up from Westerland, in northern Germany, to attack British warships in the Firth of Forth near Edinburgh, Scotland. The German leaders thought that Scotland was being defended only by a small contingent of outdated Gloster Gladiator biplane fighters. They were wrong!

Instead, two Spitfire Mk I-equipped squadrons, 602 and 603, were operating out of Drem and Turnhouse. They were there to protect British shipping in the area, which included the prized HMS *Hood*. Germany's blunder that day, during several fierce engagements, cost the Luft-waffe several Ju 88s and a number of He 111s. But still to come were the first of many meetings with the two best propeller-driven fighters Germany produced during the war, the Messerschmitt 109 and the Focke-Wulf 190.

Before the United States entered into the war, American volunteer fighter pilots were already combat veterans in three RAF Eagle Squadrons—the 71st, 121st, and 133rd. And

During the spring and summer of 1941, legendary legless ace Douglas Bader led the Tangmere Fighter Wing in Spitfires that carried his initials, DB. This one, with no 20-mm cannon, was one of the few Mk VAs built. Bader preferred maneuvering to very short range before pressing the gun button, and refused to fly cannon-armed Spitfires for some time. *Goulding via Alfred Price*

WAAF mechanics strap the pilot into a No. 411 (Canadian) Spitfire IIA at Digby in October 1941. The Spitfire's small size worked for it in many ways, yielding more maneuverability and the possibility of not being spotted so soon in the sky by enemy pilots. One didn't fly it so much as wear it. *Public Archives of Canada via Alfred Price*

Pilot Officer Gene Potter, along with his ground crew, poses on a No. 71 (Eagle) Squadron Spitfire IIB at North Weald in 1941. The Eagle Squadrons were manned by Americans who volunteered to fly for England before the U.S. entered the war. Flying both Hurricanes and Spitfires, the Eagles provided excellent operational depth for USAAF units into which they would later transfer. *Salkeld via Alfred Price*

when the U.S. joined the fray, these three squadrons were transferred to the U.S. Army Air Forces, forming the 4th Fighter Group ("Fourth but First"), which grew into Europe's mightiest aerial armada—the Eighth Air Force. Interestingly, the 4th Fighter Group has the distinction of being the only U.S. Air Force unit that can trace its history back to another country.

Flying and fighting with Spitfires exclusively before their subsequent transitions to the Republic P-47 Thunderbolt and North American P-51 Mustang, the 4th FG (with its squadrons redesignated the 334th, 335th, and 336th) was one of the record-setters throughout the air war in Europe. The 4th, at first, operated Spitfire Mk IBs, and then Mk VBs until 10 March 1943, while it was based at Debden Aerodrome, some 45 miles north of London.

It was much earlier, on 19 September 1940, when the first three American volunteers arrived in Great Britain to man and officially form the first RAF Eagle Squadron—No. 71. No. 121 Eagle Squadron was formed on 14 May 1941, and No. 133 Eagle Squadron was established on 1 August

Many Spitfires were purchased by towns, companies, and other private entities, then "presented" to the RAF. This brand-new Mk IIB presentation airframe, "Sumbawa," gets a final going over at the factory before being flown away to an operational unit. *Alfred Price*

1941. On 27 August 1941, while piloting a Spitfire Mk VB, RAF Pilot William R. Dunn (assigned to No. 71 Eagle Squadron) became the first American ace of World War II, when he downed his fifth and sixth enemy aircraft over Lille, France.

After the Battle of Britain had reached its climax, the ever-increasing number of RAF Spitfire-equipped groups continued to fly day-to-day and night-to-night area- and point-defense combat missions over and all around England. And just as soon as the newer and better versions of the Spitfire appeared and entered into battle, many Spitfire-equipped units started to leave the relative safety of their home bases, to offer themselves to do whatever it took to win the war with the Axis. This began with deployments to places like Malta, the Western Desert of North Africa, Australia and New Zealand, Burma, India, Sicily, and Italy. These places, of course, do not count the many other aerial battles that were fought over and around much closer places like Bel-

Serving in smaller numbers than in Europe, the Spitfire went to war in the China-Burma-India Theater and the Pacific with an enthusiastic band of pilots, including veteran ETO ace Ginger Lacey. This No. 54 Squadron, RAF, Mk VC at Darwin, Australia, in 1943, has the large Vokes tropical filter under the nose, which was also standard fit in the Western Desert of North Africa. *Alfred Price*

Another tropical-filtered Spitfire VC sits at readiness in the Mediterranean with No. 1 Squadron, South African Air Force, which had been fighting hard right along with its RAF sister units. The filter certainly cut down on the aircraft's performance, in both available engine power and speed, but the only alternative was engines quickly worn out by sand. *John Fawcett*

The 31st Fighter Group, one of the first fighter units with the fledgling U.S. Eighth Army Air Force in England, was equipped with reverse lend-lease Spitfire Vs at Westhampnett in the summer of 1942. By the end of the year, the group, along with several others, was transferred to North Africa, leaving the Eighth's new bomber offensive to fend for itself. *VMI Collection*

gium, Denmark, France, the Netherlands, Scotland, Ireland, Russia, and Germany itself.

In some of these aerial battles, including the "Rhubard" and "Circus" operations above Europe during 1941 and 1942, as many as 500 fighter aircraft would participate in a single sweep. The RAF, for the most part, fielded Mk II and Mk V Spitfires.

When the United States entered into the war after Japan's surprise attack on Pearl Harbor on 7 December 1941, the fighting that had been going on in Europe was already more than two years old. And in addition to the American volunteers in RAF Eagle Squadrons that were operating Spitfires out of England, a large contingent of other pilots from friendly air forces had also been assigned to RAF units. Many of these pilots operated Spitfires. Among the friendly nations that offered their pilots to the RAF were Belgium, France, Poland, Norway, the Netherlands, Canada, Russia, Yugoslavia, and Denmark. When some of these overrun countries were retaken by

Yugoslav partisans get some hands-on training with RAF Mk Vs in Italy before receiving their own Spitfires for operations in the Balkans. The Yugoslavians operated several different British types but almost every pilot's favorite was the Spitfire. Away from fixed hangers and equipment, field maintenance was never easy, but it always seemed to get done. *USAF*

A well-worn 309th Squadron, 31st Fighter Group, Mk V sits at readiness at Membury Aerodrome, England, on 15 March 1943, when the Eighth Air Force was about to send its first Thunderbolts into combat. The Spitfire had only enough range to escort bombers across the English Channel before being forced to turn around. As a result, it could not support the American daylight bomber offensive. *USAF*

the allied forces—Belgium, for example—these friendly air forces returned home with their Spitfires to continue the fight.

For more than two years then, these U.S. volunteers and the other friendly air forces personnel fought the axis in Europe before the war actually became an all-out world war. Especially dreaded was the Luftwaffe, which was a completely separate and independent military entity on a basis of full equality with Germany's army and navy. The Luftwaffe's mission was to deliver short, swift, relatively light strikes—the kind that had been optimized to stagger its enemy and to leave it helpless against immediate follow-up strikes with tanks and motorized troop divisions. The Junkers Ju 87 dive bomber was one such strike weapon operated by the Luftwaffe.

The Ju 87 Stuka was an all-metal, low-wing monoplane of cantilever construction with a top speed of only 240 miles per hour; that is, at least 150 miles per hour slower than one of its most feared adversaries—the Spitfire.

It was not until after the Battle of Britain that the Ju 87 Stuka dive bombers were really put to the test. Having already performed very well on the European continent, where in the beginning they did not come up against any modern fighters such as the Spitfire, the Ju 87s got away with cold-blooded murder. They had a serious weakness, however. With very little defensive armament (a single machine gun in the aft cockpit), when they were attacked from below, they were sitting ducks. But of course, after the battle, much more formidable German combat aircraft appeared, such as the aforementioned Me 109.

Powered by a Daimler Benz engine that ultimately produced more than 2,000 horsepower, the Me 109 was armed with six rapid-firing, heavy-caliber machine guns. Extremely maneuverable and agile, the 375-plus-miles-per-hour fighter was a serious challenger to all of the allied pursuit-interceptor aircraft, including the Spitfire. Their flying qualities were nearly equal, with a slight edge going to the Spitfire, because it was better than the

The 52nd Fighter Group was the second USAAF unit to receive Spitfires, flying fighter sweeps in England and with the 12th Air Force in the Mediterranean, before transitioning to P-51 Mustangs in the spring of 1944. These mechanics are taking no chances during an engine run-up. The tail is tied down, but two sit on the horizontal stabilizers, just in case the aircraft might nose over. Without restraining the tail, a Spitfire would nose over at half power or less. The wings also have RAF roundels on them—parts were scavenged from whatever source was available. *Alfred Price*

The Allied landings at Salerno in September 1943 were hazardous in more ways than one. American gunners mistook this 307th Squadron, 31st Fighter Group, Spitfire V for a German fighter and shot it down. Fortunately, the pilot only got a slight scratch on the back of his hand while bellying in on the surf in front of this LST, unloading vehicles of the 817th Engineer Aviation Battalion. *USAF*

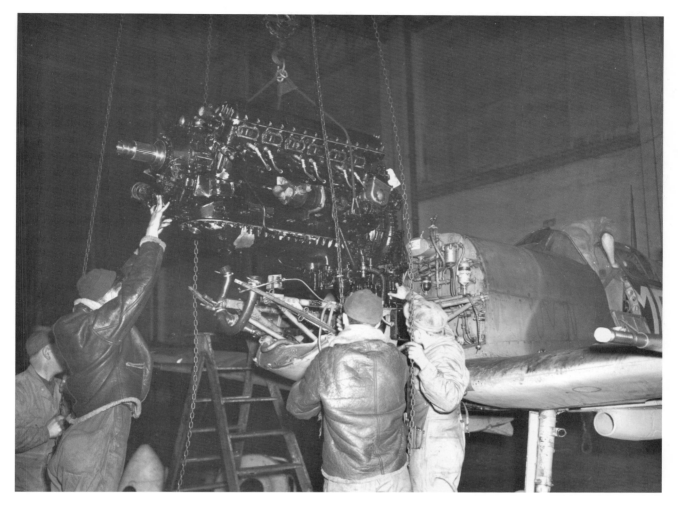

Mechanics pull the Rolls-Royce Merlin from a 336th Squadron, 4th Fighter Group, Mk V at Audley End, England, in April 1943, just as the group was transitioning to P-47 Thunderbolts. Made up of former Eagle Squadron personnel, the 4th was sad to see its Spitfires go in favor of the massive Republic fighter, but the war was taking them deeper into enemy territory than the Spitfire could go. *USAF*

Me 109 at stalling speed and in high-altitude dog-fighting. But one of the worst nightmares for the Spitfire was yet to come, in the form of the Focke-Wulf 190. Powered by the Junkers Jumo engine of more than 2,000 horsepower and capable of 425 miles per hour, the F-W 190 was nothing less than a hellraiser to the allied forces.

The F-W 190s were more than adequately armed and dangerous, and near equal to the Spitfire in altitude, speed, range, maneuverability, and agility. Of all the Luftwaffe fighters it faced, the F-W 190 was the Spitfire's most formidable foe. In post-war comparisons, almost in every instance, the 190s and Spitfires ran neck and neck.

Having successfully defended their home territories for more than two years, and with ever-grow-

ing numbers of Spitfires rolling off their production lines, this became the proper time to deploy the Spitfires elsewhere in the world to help put a stop to Hitler's unwanted advances. Thus a new phase, a visit to Malta by the British forces, ensued.

Even though Hitler had shaken the heart of England quite thoroughly, he had failed in his attempt to shatter it. Presuming England would next try to establish a naval foothold in the Mediterranean area to attack his forces in North Africa, then Sicily and Italy, Hitler turned his attention to that theater. In January 1941, the Luftwaffe unexpectedly flew out of Sicily and caused extensive damage on Malta and to the British fleet.

Over a year later, a sparse 15 Spitfire Mk VB fighters were delivered to Malta on 7 March 1942

During a sweep over North Africa, this 5th Squadron, 52nd Fighter Group, Spitfire VC was hit by German flak. The pilot managed to get it back to home base. It was too far gone to keep, so it became a salvage queen, used to keep other aircraft flying. The American flag under the VF codes was applied to keep friendly gunners from shooting at the Spitfires by mistake. *USAF*

Maj. Virgil C. Fields, CO of the 307th Squadron, 31st Fighter Group, eases into the cockpit of his Spitfire VIII at Nettuno, Italy, on 2 February 1944, during the landing at Anzio. An ace with six kills, one of the great and well-loved leaders in the unit, Fields was shot down and killed by Me 109s over Anzio just four days later. (USAF)

Servicing fighters in the field wasn't easy. These 308th Squadron, 31st Fighter Group, mechanics use 55-gallon drums with hand pumps to top up this Spitfire VIII at their Italian base. This wasn't too bad when it was warm, but in winter the procedure became excruciatingly long. *John Fawcett*

on board a Royal Navy aircraft carrier, the HMS *Eagle*. These Mk VBs were actually launched from the carrier and flown to their assigned base of operation.

Some six months later, in early September 1942, three squadrons of Mk VBs were on station in the western desert of North Africa. And to defend Darwin, Australia, from increasing Japanese bombardments, RAF Squadron No. 54's Spitfire Mk Vs began to arrive in February 1943, becoming the first Spitfires to operate in the South Pacific theater. Also equipped with Mk Vs, RAF Squadrons Nos. 136, 607, and 615 had begun to arrive in October 1943, to initiate combat operations in Burma.

Starting more than a year earlier, on 26 July 1942, the U.S. Army Air Forces' 31st Fighter Group—equipped with Spitfire Mk VB fighters, flew its first six sorties, with the loss of one plane. Then in support of the Dieppe, France, raid on 19 August, the Eighth Air Force's 31st FG flew 123 combat missions, but downed only one enemy airplane—an F-W 190. Although the 31st FG was able to boast of getting the first USAAF victory in Europe, eight American-flown Spitfire

Mk VBs were shot down that day.

With this disaster fresh on its mind, the 31st FG (comprising the 307th, 308th, and 309th Fighter Squadrons), instantly realized that its lack of combat experience had been paramount to its defeat. It was time for agonizing reappraisal and the 31st FG knew it. Worse yet, liking their reverse lend-lease Spitfires much more than their previously assigned Bell P-39 Airacobras and Curtiss P-40 Warhawks, the pilots of the 31st FG wondered if they could have performed better during their defeat with either the P-39s or P-40s they had originally trained on. Even though they were more used to their earlier fighters, they agreed at last that it did not matter all that much which fighter they were flying. In the final analysis, it was their lack of combat experience that had made the difference. Remember, when the 31st FG first entered into the fray, its enemies from Germany already had almost three years of combat experience. But as time moved on, whether they flew Spitfires or North American P-51 Mustangs—which they transitioned to in 1943—the 31st FG and its three Fighter Squadrons did an admirable job.

Smoking a cigarette, not in the least concerned with fuel fumes, a 307th Squadron, 31st Fighter Group, ground crewman prepares an external fuel tank for the Spitfire Mk VIII behind him. The VIII usually had extended wingtips and, more often than not, a pointed rudder as well as a retractable tailwheel to improve high-altitude performance. This aircraft was ridden pretty hard during its time in Italy. *John Fawcett*

The 31st and the 52nd fighter groups, had trained in and operated Bell P-39s and Curtiss P-40s. But since neither one of these fighter aircraft had enough range to fly across the Atlantic, both groups rode over on troop ships and received their new Spitfires after their arrival.

Another Eighth Air Force fighter group, the 52nd FG and its three squadrons (the 2nd, 4th, and 5th), also operated Spitfire Mk VB fighters prior to its changeover to P-51s.

Later, the 31st and 52nd FGs were reassigned to the 12th Air Force in the Mediterranean, to participate in Operation Torch, the allied invasion of French North Africa, which began on 8 November 1942.

The 4th FG of the Eighth Air Force remained on English soil partly because it had been there all along as dedicated American volunteer combat outfits in the three RAF Eagle Squadrons. And when the 4th FG was directed to trade in its highly respected Spitfires for newly arriving Republic P-47 Thunderbolts, it has been rumored, it balked at the plan. In truth, since

they had been flying and fighting in Spitfires long before America's entry into the war, they hated to part with their Spitfires.

As an aside, it is most interesting, considering all of the different lend-lease warbirds that had been sent to England from the United States in the war, that three USAAF fighter groups flew in and fought alongside the immortal Spitfire, a foreign-made warbird, from 1942 to 1944, marking the first such action since World War I. And other than the U.S. Navy's procurement of a number of Israeli-made jet fighters to be used in an aggressor squadron in the 1980s, this has not happened again.

One U.S. Spitfire Mk VB pilot, retired USAF Colonel Alvin M. Cole (Al), who served with the 335th FS of the 4th FG (formerly RAF Squadron Eagle Squadron No. 121), wrote: "Though we did transition later to P-47s and P-51s, I'll always have the very most respect for the now quaint Spitfire. Especially for the reasons as follows: Firstly, I flew 152 combat missions in two versions of the Spitfire (Mk IB and Mk VB), and in

With the "trolley ac" or auxiliary power unit plugged in, two 52nd Fighter Group pilots prepare to start a Spitfire at Palermo, Sicily, in September 1943. All Marks of the Spitfire were just about the easiest of wartime aircraft to start—fuel cock on, mixture forward, magnetos on, prime four strokes, push the starter and booster coil buttons simultaneously. It was a rare bird that didn't catch in two blades, then run like a sewing machine. *John Fawcett*

addition to their great agility in an all-out furball [dogfight], they didn't lose as much energy [speed] as our P-47s; secondly, they didn't become anywhere as near unstable [wobbly] as our own P-51s tried to do after bomb drops; and lastly, following my initiation with fighter-type planes in the form of the P-39, and after only a short time getting used to it, my reassignment to a Spitfire was a godsend."

Royal Air Force Spitfires in Action

In April 1942, after it had first gathered its strength at Malta, RAF Squadron No. 145 became the first Desert Air Force unit to become fully operational in North Africa. Initially based at Heliopolis, Egypt, with standard Spitfire Mk VB fighters, No. 145 Squadron was soon re-equipped with tropicalized Mk VBs that featured the Vokes air-filtration system in deep, chin-type fairings under their noses. After moving northward to Gambut on 1 June, the No. 145 Squadron flew its first combat mission in sup-

port of Hawker Hurricanes that were being used as dive bombers. And by the end of June 1942, No. 145 Squadron had been joined by Nos. 92 and 601, which created RAF Wing No. 244 of Group No. 211, which worked in concert with Hurricanes.

These Spitfire-equipped squadrons and numerous others played a significant role in North Africa, Sicily, and Italy, and most importantly at the time, substantially aided in the allied invasions in these same areas of combat.

About a year later, in the early days of July 1943, when the allies started their invasions of Sicily, Italy, and the Balkans, Spitfires and RAF-operated U.S.-made P-40s combined to fly 1,092 combat missions on the first day of the invasion of southern Europe.

Also during 1943, numerous other Spitfire units were fighting almost everywhere in northwestern Europe. Spitfires first started to serve as fighter-bombers during their attacks upon such strategic targets as V-1 and V-2 construction and

launch sites. The Spitfires were usually armed with a single belly-mounted 500-pound general-purpose bomb, and in some cases, with two smaller 250-pound bombs under either wing.

Any modern conflict creates a dire need to gather credible intelligence on enemy locations and movements. In this light, due to its increasing speed and altitude capabilities, numerous Spitfires had been either designed from the outset, or modified, to serve as both armed and unarmed photographic reconnaissance and/or mapping aircraft. And these, like their dedicated fighter counterparts, did nothing less than a marvelous job for the allied intelligence community.

In the Far East and South Pacific, the Royal Australian Air Force (RAAF) and the Royal New Zealand Air Force (RNZAF) systematically used their Spitfires to account for a great deal of aerial victories over the best opposition Japan had to offer. Fighting throughout the South and Middle Pacific Ocean areas and over the China, Burma, and India (CBI) theaters of war, these

RAAF and RNZAF Spitfires proved to be more than match for the Axis aircraft.

Whether they fought in the ETO, MTO, CBI, or whatever theater, it just did not matter. For wherever they fought, the Vickers-Supermarine Spitfires excelled to make their respective Marks as dedicated combat aircraft.

Royal Navy Seafires

In their operations from the pitching, rolling, and yawing decks of numerous Royal Navy aircraft carriers, and from land bases as well, the Royal Navy's fleet of Vickers-Supermarine Seafire fighters earned their spurs in combat beginning in late 1942. This action started with Seafire Mk IB fighters assigned to Royal Navy Squadron No. 801, aboard the aircraft carrier HMS *Furious*.

After the upgraded Seafire Mk IICs started to become available to their user squadrons, most of the Mk IBs were transferred out of their front-line squadrons to be used as training aircraft. The

The rain-soaked field at Pomigliano, Naples, Italy, in December 1943 didn't seem to stop these 31st Fighter Group Spitfires from taxiing out to the runway. If pilots had been forced to wait for the mud to dry out, they would never have flown. Spitfires were particularly suited to rough field conditions, with outstanding stability on both landing and takeoff. *John Fawcett*

Seafire Mk IIC fighters, faster and more heavily armed than the Mk IB, were deployed primarily in Europe and Mediterranean theaters of operations by the summer of 1943. In both cases, they made a good showing until the even more improved Seafire Mk IIIs and Seafire Mk XVs appeared.

It was the Mk XV version of the Seafire that first encountered the notorious Mitsubishi A6M Zero fighters. Powered by the 1,000-plus-horse-

A crew chief runs up his 308th Squadron, 31st Fighter Group, Spitfire VIII at Castel Volturno, Italy, in March 1944, as the group was giving up its Spitfires for P-51B Mustangs. The squadron emblem has not been painted on the blank-white background yet. These tan and brown machines with blue undersurfaces in their American markings were among the most beautiful Spitfires of the war. *John Fawcett*

Lt. John Fawcett with the 309th Squadron, 31st Fighter Group, Mk IX Spitfire named for his wife. At the time, Fawcett was at Castel Volturno, Italy, during the fierce fighting at Anzio when so many 31st Group pilots were flying long hours and many were going down. The slight smile on this man's face covers a grim weariness common to those covering the invasion. *John Fawcett*

power Nakajima Sakae radial engine, armed with two 20-mm cannons and a pair of 7.7-mm machine guns, these 330-miles-per-hour fighters were both maneuverable and agile during air-to-air combat, despite their lack of speed. Their top speed notwithstanding, another bonus to the allies was that the Zero was not equipped with heavy self-protecting armor plating, and they were easily shot down when they were fired upon. But by the time the Royal Navy had been reasonably outfitted with its new and improved Seafire Mk XVs, the once feared and deadly Zero was no longer much of a threat. It had met its match. Moreover, due to attrition, Japan did not have many skilled combat pilots left.

The Vickers-Supermarine Seafire Mk XVs served mainly throughout the Far East. Being the Royal Navy's equal to the Royal Air Force's Griffon-powered Spitfire Mk XII, which had a maximum speed of 393 miles per hour at an altitude 18,000 feet, the Seafire Mk XVs were every bit as capable as the aforementioned version of the Spitfire.

In the Far East, three Seafire squadrons flew combat air patrols from Royal Navy aircraft car-riers, the HMS *Attacker* (No. 879 Squadron), HMS *Hunter* (No. 807 Squadron), and the HMS *Stalker* (No. 809 Squadron). Between 30 April and 2 May 1945, the Seafire Mk XVs participated in Operation Dracula, in support of the allied land-ings in Burma. Although no aerial combat ensued during this time, the Seafire Mk XVs con-tinually exhausted their ammunition in day-after-day, hour-after-after strafing runs against Japanese positions.

From this time until the two atomic bombs were dropped on Hiroshima and Nagasaki, on 6 and 9 August 1945, which of course brought about V-J Day on 2 September, Royal Navy Seafires were employed for various duties, which included dive-bombing, strafing, and escorting other planes on photographic reconnaissance flights.

The Mk XV was the last version of the Seafire to see combat duty in World War II, their last mission coming on 15 August, when Mk XVs of Nos. 887 and 894 Squadrons sent eight Zeros into the waters off Tokyo without a single loss.

The four final versions of the carrier-based Seafire—the F Mk 17, F Mk 45, F Mk 46, and the

Lady Ellen III was the Spitfire IX assigned to John Fawcett at Castel Volturno, Italy, when the 31st Fighter Group was engaged in the heavy fighting over the Anzio beachhead. The two groups of American pilots in the MTO flying Spitfires, the 31st and 52nd, loved their sleek Spitfires with a passion and hated to let them go for Mustangs. *John Fawcett*

FR Mk 47, would see combat action later during the Malayan Emergency, from 1948 to 1951, and in the Korean War from 1950 to 1953.

Finally the Seafires, like the Spitfires, were employed by most of the same foreign users who used the Spitfire: Belgium, Burma, Czechoslovakia, Denmark, Egypt, Eire, France, Greece, Holland, Italy, Norway, Portugal, Russia, South Africa, Syria, Thailand, Turkey, and Yugoslavia.

Spitfire Aces

The Vickers-Supermarine Spitfire Mk I through Mk 24 series of low-, medium-, and high-altitude fighters, fighter-bombers, fighter-interceptors, and armed and unarmed photographic reconnaissance aircraft are dearly remembered as one of history's most formidable weapons of war. They were dedicated warplanes, which, in their fighter and interceptor roles, created numerous aces, with at least five confirmed kills each. Better yet, a number of these Spitfire aces became two-, three-, four-, five-, and even six-time aces. Near seven-time ace retired RAF Air Vice Marshal James E. Johnson (Johnnie) leads

the way, with 34 Axis aircraft destroyed, seven shared destroyed, five shared and probably destroyed, 13 shared damaged, and one shared destroyed on the ground. He earned the right to be credited as the highest-scoring Spitfire ace of the war, and in dramatic fashion, most of his aerial victories came while he was fighting against single-engine "hot dog" fighters like the Me 109 and the F-W 190. And just one of his 34 kills was a less formidable twin-engine plane, an Me 110.

Being a fighter pilot is never an easy task. This is true for several reasons: Firstly, a fighter pilot has to be an outstanding aviator; secondly, he must be a fearless warrior with the mentality of a cold-blooded killer; and lastly, though he fully intends to kill his adversary, he must retain the very highest respect for him. For he too is a dedicated fighter pilot with a job to do for his own country. This mutual respect between former fighter pilot enemies can be witnessed today at World War II anniversary functions, air shows, and the like. It was and is during these events where past foes have become fast friends. But it was a lot different during the 1939–1945 period.

Lt. Hank Hughes with Audrey, his 309th Squadron, 31st Fighter Group, Spitfire at Castel Volturno, Italy, February 1944. The late 1943 red surround on the national star and bar was supposed to have been painted over with blue by this time, but mechanics had little time to attend to the myriad markings changes which seemed to plague them. There were more important things to do. *John Fawcett*

These 52nd Fighter Group Spitfires share the field with RAF Spitfires at Palermo, Sicily, in August 1943. Cooperation between the two nations flying the same aircraft type was the norm rather than the exception, particularly at this period in the war when there weren't enough fighters to go around for the missions scheduled. *John Fawcett*

During the 1942–45 period, while for the most part they were flying later versions of the Spitfire, a number of Spitfire aces appeared. Some of these were: (1.) RAF Group Captain Colin Gray of New Zealand, with 27 destroyed; (2.) RAF Squadron Leader Neville Duke of Great Britain, with 26 destroyed; (3.) RAF Wing Commander Lance Wade of the United States, with 22 destroyed; (4.) RAF Squadron Leader Johannes LeRoux (Chris) of South Africa, with 18 destroyed; (5.) RAF Wing Commander Donald Kingaby of Great Britain, with 21 destroyed; (6.) RAF Squadron Leader Henry McLeod of Canada, with 21 destroyed; (7.) RAF Air Vice Marshal William Crawford-Compton of New Zealand, with 20 (possibly 21) destroyed; (8.) RAF Squadron Leader Raymond Hesselyn of New Zealand, with 18 (possibly 20) destroyed; (9.) RAF Group Captain Wilfred Duncan-Smith of India, with 17 destroyed; and (10.) RAF Group Captain

An RAF Spitfire VC, fitted with the massive Vokes dust filter, sits at Palermo, Sicily, in August 1943. The Mark V was the most numerous of the Spitfire versions at this period in the war. Not the best performer compared to the F-W 190 and the Me 109, it was still an excellent low-level fighter, and there were enough to give the Germans a headache. *John Fawcett*

Raymond Harries of Great Britain, with 15 destroyed.

Many other Spitfire aces appeared throughout the numerous areas of battle in which these famed fighters and their brave pilots flew and fought. While it is true that many of these aces were killed in action, many others were fortunate to survive. Yet to a man, whether he got zero kills or 30-plus, these survivors have the highest regard for one another. The reason is, to paraphrase World War II hero and movie actor Audie Murphy, they had gone "To Hell And Back."

There were many great fighter-type planes that emerged from the glowing embers of World War II, most being the standout products of the United States, the United Kingdom, Russia, Japan, Germany, and Italy. When you compare the best of the best—America's P-38 Lightning, P-47 Thunderbolt, and P-51 Mustang; Great Britain's Hurricane, Tempest, and Mosquito; Japan's Zero, Raiden, and Ki-21; Germany's Me 109, F-W 190, and Me 262; and Russia's YaK-9, MiG-11, and La-5—there is no hesitation in adding two more to this distinguished list: Britain's Spitfire and Seafire.

Another Mark VC at Palermo has had the round bump-wing leading-edge fairing for a second set of wing cannons removed and smoothed over. The V, especially when fitted with the drag-inducing, power-robbing Vokes filter, needed every bit of performance it could get. Pilots often asked their ground crew to remove as much weight as possible, even if it meant having less firepower. *John Fawcett*

VICKERS-SUPERMARINE SPITFIRE SERIES: MK I THROUGH MK 24

During some 12 years of design, development, and production of the Spitfire series of aircraft, Vickers-Supermarine fathered no less than 24 major variants of the Spitfire, and a number of minor ones. They served as fighters, fighter-bombers, fighter-interceptors, and both armed and unarmed photographic reconnaissance and mapping aircraft—a total of 20,351 of them in all.

The legendary Spitfire earned the distinction of being the only allied fighter to remain in production throughout the entire war against the Axis, which for Great Britain began on 3 September 1939 and ended on 2 September 1945—six full years, minus one day.

Spitfire Vs of the 12th and 109th Squadrons, 67th Tac Recon Group, form up over England during the unit's stay at Membury, England, from late 1942 to November 1943. These squadrons rarely flew in this kind of strength, since their primary mission was individual aircraft low-level tactical reconnaissance, a combination of taking pictures and shooting up enemy targets of opportunity. *USAF*

These immortal fighters, which had helped to stop the advances of Germany's Luftwaffe at the English Channel during the Battle of Britain, were manufactured by Supermarine Aviation Works, a division of Vickers (Aviation) Limited (later Vickers-Armstrongs Limited) in factories at Castle Bromwich, Southampton, Swindon, and Winchester, after their initial by-hand assemblies at Eastleigh. Further, and importantly, there were numerous subcontractors throughout all of England that participated in their construction processes. In part, these included Aircraft Limited, Pobjoy Powerplants and General Aircraft Limited (wings), Aero Motors Limited (elevators and ailerons), General Electric of England (wingtips), and Folland Aircraft Limited (empennage).

With this, the major Spitfire variants are now discussed.

Spitfire Mk I/Mk IA/Mk IB: On 3 June 1936, less than three months after the inaugural flight of the baby-blue-colored Type 300 prototype, the first of what would be many production contracts for 310 Spitfire Mk Is was awarded to Vickers-Supermarine by the British Air Ministry. And with that first high-volume contract, R. J. Mitchell's hard work had begun to pay off. Initially armed with four Browning .303 machine guns as the Mk I—being increased to eight guns

This recce Spitfire PR.IV was critical to the Allies on Malta in January 1943. Malta was one of the few forward bases from which Britain could launch reconnaissance missions over German-held territory. The danger the few Spitfire photo pilots faced was well portrayed in the 1953 Alec Guinness film *Malta Story*. Bicycles were the norm, as the besieged island could spare fuel only for combat. *USAF*

In April and May 1942, the American aircraft carrier USS *Wasp* carried Spitfire VCs to Malta during the island's desperate hours. These aircraft flew off the carrier's deck direct to the fields on Malta and began combat operations immediately. Here a deck officer flags off one of those much-needed Spitfires. *National Archives*

as they became available for the Mk IA, these first production Spitfires were powered by either the Rolls-Royce Merlin II or III engines of 1,020 or 1,030 horsepower.

As it happened, the first production Spitfire Mk I airplane (K9788) rolled out in July 1938, and made its first flight shortly thereafter. Spitfire Mk I Number One and Number Two (K9789) remained with their manufacturer for exhaustive air worthiness trials, as production moved forward. After its manufacturer's trials, the third airplane was ferried to Royal Air Force No. 12 Group, No. 19 Squadron at Duxford on 4 August 1938 for the Spitfire's initial military trials. No. 19 Squadron, which at the time was still operating its tired fleet of outdated biplane Gloster Gladiators, was able to transition to their new Mk I monoplanes by 19 December 1938, in a little more than four months.

The Spitfire Mk I fighters featured relatively small and light airframes, literally wrapped around their massive Rolls-Royce Merlin II/III engines. And as they began to enter into group and squadron service as both daytime and nighttime point- and area-defense fighter-interceptors, it became readily apparent that they were going to be exceptional aircraft.

While on alert in England, most Spitfires were parked in blast-proof revetments, like these for No. 603 Squadron. Standard during the Battle of Britain, these revetments were quite effective in protecting aircraft from most bomb explosions other than the rare direct hit. *Chidgey/Garbett via Alfred Price*

• • •

Spitfire Mk I/IA/IB Specifications

Wing span	36 feet, 10 inches
Length	29 feet, 11 inches
Height	12 feet, 7 3/4 inches
Powerplant	1,020-horsepower Rolls-Royce Merlin II (Mk I/IA); 1,030-horsepower Rolls-Royce Merlin III (Mk IB) with single-stage superchargers
Armament	Four .303 machine guns (Mk I); eight .303 machine guns (Mk IA "A" wing); two 20-mm cannons and four .303 machine guns (Mk IB "B" wing)
Maximum speed	355 miles per hour at 19,000 feet
Maximum range	450 miles on 85 gallons of fuel
Rate of climb	2,420 feet per minute (6.2 minutes to 15,000 feet)
Service ceiling	34,000 feet

• • •

Few aircraft could take on maneuverable Japanese fighters like the Zero and Oscar one-on-one—but the Spitfire was one that could. Most Allied pilots were told never to dogfight with the Japanese, but that didn't hold for men like these in front of their No. 150 Squadron Mk VIII in Burma. Though Spitfires were few in number in the CBI and the Pacific, they were much valued. *Alfred Price*

Spitfire Mk IIA/IIB: With the advent of the greater-horsepower Rolls-Royce Merlin XII engine, equipped with a two-stage, rather than a single-stage, gear-driven supercharger, the Spitfire Mk II series appeared.

The Spitfire Mk IIA version, configured with the "A" wing armament, was near identical to its predecessor Mk IA counterpart. And the Mk IIB version, with the "B" wing armament, was very similar to its earlier Mk IB relation; that is, it was armed with four Browning .303 machine guns (1,200 total rounds of ammunition or 300 rounds per gun) in can-type magazines and two British-made Hispano 20-mm cannons (with 120 total rounds of ammunition or 60 rounds per cannon) in drum-type magazines. The pair of cannons had replaced the two inboard machine guns in either wing. The first Spitfire Mk II (P7280) made its first flight in late summer of 1940.

The tapered wingtips and retractable tailwheel fitted to Spitfire Mk VIIIs are more than evident on these No. 417 (Canadian) Squadron aircraft in Italy. Those who flew the VIIIs considered them wonderful aircraft with excellent high-altitude performance. Their one drawback was the same most Spitfires suffered from—lack of range. *Public Archives of Canada via Alfred Price*

A Free French Air Force Spitfire Mk IX cruises near the Mediterranean coastline in 1944. The French were given a number of different American and British types to continue fighting while their country was occupied. Quite often the aircraft were close to being worn out, but that didn't stop pilots from using them to their limits. *USAF*

Spitfire Mk IIA/IIB Specifications

Wing span	36 feet, 10 inches
Length	29 feet, 11 inches
Height	12 feet, 8 inches
Powerplant	1,040-horsepower Rolls-Royce Merlin XII with two-stage supercharger; cartridge rather than electrical start system
Armament	Mk IIA had eight Browning .303 machine guns; Mk IIB had four .303 guns and two Hispano 20-mm cannons
Maximum speed	355 miles per hour
Maximum range	425 miles with 124 gallons internal fuel
Rate of climb	2,900 feet per minute at sea level
Service ceiling	34,000 feet

Two ground crewmen change the film magazine on a reconnaissance camera before refitting it to a No. 225 Squadron Spitfire in Italy. Like so many other Mediterranean Spitfire units, 225 was primarily engaged in tactical reconnaissance at low level, which rarely afforded the opportunity to engage enemy aircraft. *USAF*

A flight of 313 Squadron Spitfire Mk IXs visited the 4th Fighter Group at Debden, England, in 1944, after being unable to get into their own base in bad weather. In spite of the miserable weather, England was an ideal operating area, due to the dozens of airfields which were within miles of each other—"Just fly in a straight line and in a few minutes you'd fly across a field." *F. M. Grove*

One of the many Mk IXs originally ordered as Vs runs up in Italy before a sortie. Two crewmen pull the trolley ac away, while another removes the power cable from the APU receptacle on the right side of the engine cowling. The rough field was absolutely no problem for a Spitfire pilot. *John Fawcett*

Spitfire Mk III: Now came the even more powerful and reliable 1,390-horsepower Rolls-Royce Merlin Mk XX engine, boosted by a two-stage supercharger, which promised and delivered much improved performance at all altitudes. Therefore, to accommodate the fresh powerplant from R-R, Vickers-Supermarine created the Spitfire Mk III prototype (N3297). And on 16 March 1940, under the guidance of test pilot Jeffrey Quill, the new type of Spitfire fighter made a successful first test hop. Other improvements enjoyed by the Spitfire Mk III included a reduction in overall wing span to 30 feet, 6 inches to improve the plane's roll rate, and an increase in overall length to 30 feet, 4 inches to offset the plane's lower aspect ratio and to increase the fuselage's fineness ratio. Unfortunately, because the Merlin XX engine was first being produced for the Royal Air Force Bomber Command, it was not yet available to the Royal Air Force Fighter Command—specifically, to the Spitfire. The result: After 1,000 Spitfire Mk IIIs had been

ordered, the type had to be canceled. Fortunately, however, the improvements which were to be incorporated on the Spitfire Mk III would again surface at a later date in the form of the heavily manufactured Spitfire Mk V series.

Spitfire Mk IV: Before the Merlin-powered Mk V series emerged, yet another version of the Spitfire appeared—the short-lived Mk IV. This variant was created to investigate the feasibility of incorporating Rolls-Royce's new Griffon engine, which was a larger, heavier, and more powerful version of the Merlin engine. To this end, Vickers-Supermarine built two Spitfire Mk IV prototypes, which performed well during testing. But once more, the new engine was not yet available to the Spitfire breed, and the proposed Mk IV was shelved. But the new Griffon engine held immense promise, as the prototype Mk IVs had hit 370-plus miles per hour in level flight, reached 39,600 feet, and could climb at 4,200 feet per minute.

During the American 5th Army's assault on the center of the Italian Gothic Line in the fall of 1944, these South African Spitfires, usually carrying 500-pound bombs, supported the effort. The light Spitfires were quite nimble at ground support, even though they could not carry the weight in bombs usually borne by 12th Air Force Thunderbolts. *USAF*

Spitfire PR Mk IV: Ultimately, almost every high-speed fighter-type aircraft gets drafted for dedicated photographic reconnaissance and mapping duties. Thus it was with the Spitfire PR Mk IV aircraft. It should be noted, however, that while the PR Mk IV was the first production photo-recce version of the Spitfire, earlier Mk Is and IIs had been used after modification in the field; these nonproduction photo-recce Spitfires were first designated as the "A" through "G" photo birds before the PR Mk IV appeared.

To produce the unarmed Spitfire PR Mk IV, Vickers-Supermarine took newly built Spitfire Mk V airframes and, instead of arming them, installed cameras into their aft fuselage sections. And, since there were no armament in the wings, two additional 33-gallon fuel tanks were installed in the leading edges of the reconfigured wings to increase range. And to propel them at high-speed over enemy installations, they were powered by the 1,100-horsepower Rolls-Royce Merlin 46 or subsequent series engines for low-, medium-, and high-altitude operations.

For its photo-recce operations, the PR Mk IV was equipped with various combinations of F8 (20-inch focal length), F24 (14-inch focal length), and F52 (36-inch focal length) cameras which were mounted in the aft fuselage and wings. The PR Mk IV was never armed. Primarily powered by the Merlin 46 or 50 engines, they were the fastest photo-recce birds of the Royal Air Force, capable of 380-plus miles per hour at best altitude.

Spitfire Mk V Series

Spitfire Mk VA/VB/VC: The Spitfire Mk VA, Mk VB, and Mk VC series were beefed-up Mk I and Mk II airframes that had been strengthened to accept the heavier Rolls-Royce Merlin 45 and 50 engines. As their development programs proceeded, the Spitfire Mk Vs underwent a hoard of improvements and modifications. As a result, the Mk Vs were employed in numerous ways throughout their tenure. The Spitfire Mk V series enjoyed the largest production run to that time, topping out at 6,464 examples.

Support of armies in the field meant a great deal of flying from forward bases, usually having nothing more than a bare strip. Pilots like these were forced to do their own mission planning in the open, then go after the targets without much help. The 20-mm cannons were quite effective against anything on the ground, except tanks.

Spitfire Mk VA: The first of 94 Spitfire Mk VA fighter aircraft (X4922), piloted by Jeffrey Quill, made a successful first flight on 20 February 1941. Powered by the newer and more powerful 1,440-horsepower Rolls-Royce Merlin 45 engine turning a two-stage supercharger, armed with the "A" wing (eight .303 machine guns), an early production Mk VA hit a maximum speed of 350 miles per hour in level flight at 15,000 feet. But with the new Merlin 45, after the early gremlins were eliminated, later production Mk Vs easily flew at 370 miles per hour or faster at best altitude, which was 20,000 feet for this type.

Spitfire Mk VA (Tropicalized): The tropicalized version of the Spitfire Mk VA was powered by the high-altitude version of the Merlin 45, the Merlin 46. It featured a large, ungainly undernose filter-equipped carburetor air scoop for use in sandy and dusty areas, such as the African deserts. Other than its Merlin 46 engine and its ugly-looking chin scoop, this version of the Spitfire was identical to the Mk VA.

• • •

Spitfire Mk VA Specifications

Wing span	36 feet, 10 inches
Length	29 feet, 11 inches
Height	10 feet
Powerplant	1,440-horsepower Rolls-Royce Merlin 45 (or Merlin 46 in the tropicalized version) with a two-stage supercharger
Armament	Eight Browning .303 machine guns
Maximum speed	370-plus miles per hour
Maximum range	425 miles on internal fuel
Rate of climb	3,350 feet per minute at sea level
Service ceiling	36,700 feet (38,200 feet for tropicalized version)

• • •

A 306 (Polish) Squadron Spitfire Mk IX warms up at Northolt during an overcast day in 1943. Expatriate pilots from many nations escaped the Germans to fly with the RAF, some forming several squadrons. The Americans had three, the Eagle Squadrons, and the Poles flew in more than one as well, helping to ease the shortage of RAF pilots at just the right time. *Alfred Price*

Spitfire Mk VB: The Spitfire Mk VB fighter was essentially a Mk VA with the "B" wing armament configuration; that is, it came equipped with four Browning .303 machine guns with 350 rounds per gun, and two 20-mm Hispano cannons with 120 rounds for each (double that of the earlier Mk IIB). In other words, the Spitfire Mk VB was a gunnery platform capable of unleashing up to 1,400 rounds of .303 bullets and as many as 240 rounds of .787-inch projectiles on enemy targets.

As with the Spitfire VA, there came a tropicalized Mk VB, too. One version of the tropicalized Spitfire VB employed the improved Aboukir air-filtration system, developed by a Royal Air Force maintenance unit at Aboukir, Egypt. The Aboukir system used a much smaller air scoop, decreasing parasite drag on the aircraft.

In all 3,923 Spitfire Mk VB fighters were built, making it the first mass-produced version of the Spitfire.

Some Mk VBs were completed with a shortened wing span of 32 feet, 6 inches—a reduction of 4 feet, 4 inches. To do this without major surgery, the aircraft were completed without their standard wingtips, and the open-ended wings were fitted with replacement fairings to justify the required aerodynamic cohesion of the aircraft. This simple modification increased wing loading and overall maneuverability and agility. It should be noted, however, this was not a very popular modification among the men who had to fly and fight in these lowered aspect ratio Spitfires.

Another version of the Spitfire Mk VB was the LF VB—the LF prefix meaning the aircraft had been optimized for low-altitude operations. This version was powered by the 1,585-horsepower Rolls-Royce Merlin 50M engine, which gave the type a pretty impressive top speed of 350 miles per hour during low-altitude combat activities.

Spitfire Mk VC: First appearing in October 1941, the Spitfire Mk VC fighter featured the new Universal or "C" wing armament arrangement, which could be reconfigured to accept eight Browning .303 machine guns, four .303 machine guns, and two Hispano 20-mm cannons, or four 20-mm cannons. The Mk VC's wing

Sgt. Tadeusz Szymkowiak happily poses for the camera on his No. 303 (Polish) Squadron Spitfire in mid-1943. The aircraft's cockpit was so small, an access door had to be designed to fold out to get in. A crowbar was fitted to this door just in case it jammed, enabling the pilot to pry himself out or break the canopy Perspex. *Alfred Price*

was strengthened to use these varying armament loads. And to improve its taxiing, take off, and landing stabilities, the outward-retracting landing gear struts were raked forward 2 inches. But other than its structurally stronger "C" wing and its 1,470-plus-horsepower Merlin 50 engine, the Spitfire Mk VCs were very much like its Mk VA and Mk VB counterparts.

Vickers-Supermarine proceeded to build a total of 2,447 Spitfire Mk VC fighters. When this is combined with the Mk VB total of 3,923, it can be said that the Mk V series was the first genuinely successful version of the Spitfire.

In summary, the Spitfire Mk VA, Mk VB, and Mk VC series of fighters appeared with either clipped or unclipped wings, at least nine different models of the Rolls-Royce Merlin engine (45, 45M, 46, 50, 50A, 50M, 55, 55M, and 56), a vastly improved air filtration system for the tropicalized version of the Mk VB, and three completely

With the Griffon-powered Spitfires came a massive jump in performance, making these versions among the fastest propeller-driven fighters of the war. Wing Commander R. C. Waddell led 39 Wing, 2nd Tactical Air Force, in this FR.XIV as the war drew to a close in 1945. The sleek fighter carries his initials, a custom followed by most RAF wing commanders. *Alfred Price*

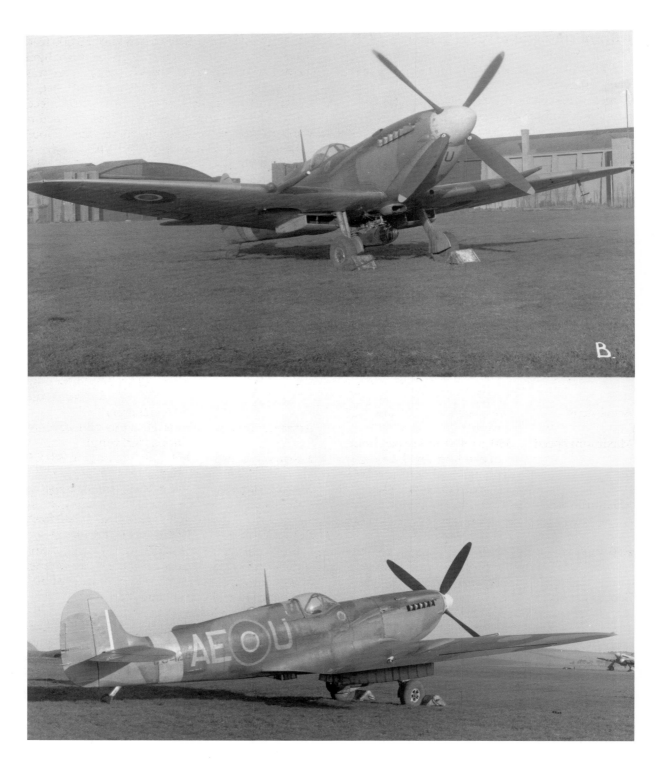

When necessary, the Spitfire could carry quite a bit more weight than original design specs called for. The 1,000-pound bomb hung under this No. 402 Squadron, RCAF, Mk IX was standard during the Normandy breakout and the subsequent push toward Germany in 1944, although the Typhoon in the background was more noted for its ground support work. *Alfred Price*

different armament packages in their respective "A," "B" and "C" wing applications.

The Merlin 45M, 50M, and 55M power-plants allowed for optimum low-altitude performance, while the Merlin 50A and 56 engines were best suited to high-altitude operations.

In all, though production records vary, Vickers-Supermarine manufactured some 6,460 Spitfire Mk Vs of all types. Moreover, with the adoption of the Merlin 45 series engine, at least 200 Spitfire Mk Is and Mk IIs were converted to Mk V standard.

• • •

Spitfire Mk VC Specifications

Wing span	36 feet, 10 inches standard; or 32 feet, 6 inches clipped
Length	29 feet, 11 inches
Height	10 feet
Powerplant	1,440-horsepower to 1,600-horsepower Rolls-Royce Merlin 45 and 50 series of engines with two-stage superchargers
Armament	Universal ("A," "B," and "C" wings)
Maximum speed	350 to 400 miles per hour, depending on the power-plant used and its best performance altitude
Maximum range	More than 600 miles with fixed slipper-type external fuel tanks
Rate of climb	4,720 feet per minute (attained) to an altitude of 2,000 feet
Service ceiling	37,000 feet

• • •

Spitfire Mk VI: The Spitfire Mk VI was developed from the outset to serve as a pure high-altitude fighter-interceptor, and as such, it came with a fully pressurized cockpit. The prototype Spitfire Mk VI (X4942), with Jeffrey Quill at its controls, made a successful first flight on 5 July 1941. It was powered by the 1,600-horsepower Rolls-Royce Merlin 47 engine, which had been specifically engineered for high-altitude flight. During subsequent flight-test operations, the second production Spitfire Mk VI (AB200) rose to an altitude of 38,000 feet, or more than 7.2 miles above England, at which its cockpit pres-

surization system equaled a height of 28,000 feet. To increase the fighter's stability at such high altitudes, the Spitfire Mk VI's wing span was increased from 36 feet, 10 inches to 40 feet, 2 inches, and its tail height was increased to 11 feet, 2 inches. Furthermore, to obtain as much forward thrust as possible at these tremendous heights, the special-mission Mk VIs were completed with four-bladed propellers. Still, the appearance of an even better high-altitude version of the Spitfire—the Mk IX—was just around the bend. So as an interim high-altitude fighter, only 100 Mk VIs were built, while the RAF waited for its new and improved Mk IX.

• • •

Spitfire Mk VI Specifications

Wing span	40 feet, 2 inches
Length	29 feet, 11 inches
Height	11 feet, 2 inches
Powerplant	Liquid oxygen-injected 1,600-plus-horsepower Rolls-Royce Merlin 47 engine with two-stage supercharger
Armament	Four Hispano 20-mm cannons ("C" wing)
Maximum speed	264 miles per hour at 38,000 feet
Maximum range	400 miles on internal fuel
Rate of climb	240 feet per minute at 38,000 feet to 39,200 feet*
Service ceiling	39,200 feet (attained)

* Since the Spitfire Mk VI was optimized for high-altitude missions, a normal service ceiling, at which the rate of climb would be at least 500 feet per minute, became moot.

Spitfire Mk VII: The Spitfire Mk VII was likewise a dedicated high-altitude fighter-interceptor airplane. Fitted with a fully pressurized cockpit, a pointed broad-chord vertical tail (in most cases) and a retractable tailwheel, the 140 Spitfire Mk VII aircraft were powered by three different versions of the two-stage Rolls-Royce Merlin engine, the 61, 64, and 71. Some of the Mk VIIs were fitted with the longer wings employed by the Mk VI, but since they performed as well with the standard wings, most were retrofitted with the normal wings, which spanned 36 feet, 10 inches. The prototype Mk VII (AB450) made its first flight in April 1942.

One of the first aircraft to land at Alto Airfield, Corsica, in April 1944 was this No. 154 Squadron Spitfire IXC. Alto was a critical forward operating base, later well used by 57th Fighter Group Thunderbolts in keeping the Allied push going in Italy. *USAF*

• • •

Spitfire Mk VII Specifications

Wing span	36 feet, 10 inches (40 feet, 2 inches on some)
Length	30 feet
Height	11 feet, 2 inches
Powerplant	1,565-horsepower Rolls-Royce Merlin 61, or 1,710-horsepower Merlin 64, or 1,250-horsepower Merlin 71; all with two-stage superchargers
Armament	"B" wing; four Browning .303 machine guns, and two Hispano 20-mm cannons
Maximum speed	410 miles per hour at 25,000 feet
Maximum range	650 miles with 120 gallons or 1,150 miles on 210 gallons
Rate of climb	2,800 feet per minute at sea level
Service ceiling	43,000 feet

• • •

Spitfire PR/FR Mk VII: Derived from the Spitfire Mk V series of fighters, the photographic reconnaissance and mapping Spitfire PR Mk VII aircraft were both armed and unarmed. The armed versions were designated Spitfire FR Mk VII. Though primarily powered by the Rolls-Royce Merlin 45 or 46 engines, some of the armed FR Mk VIIs were powered by the low-altitude Merlin 32 engine. Some of the later production PR Mk VII airplanes were equipped with two 30-gallon external fuel tanks, and to distinguish them from their clean-wing brothers, they were redesignated as Spitfire PR Mk VIIIs.

Spitfire Mk VIII: Similar to the Spitfire Mk VII discussed above, the Spitfire Mk VIII came equipped with two integral 14-gallon wing leading-edge fuel tanks, a retractable tailwheel, a beefier airframe, shorter-length ailerons, the pointed broad-chord vertical tail, and the Rolls-Royce Merlin 66 and 70 engines. However, the Mk VIII did not come with a pressurized cockpit, and only a few of the early production models had the extended-length wings. And even though the Spitfire Mk VIII fighters did not have the benefit of cockpit pressurization, they were used in both low-altitude and limited high-altitude

An American 7th Photo Group Spitfire PR.XI, on short final at Mount Farm, England, has flaps down and power back. The Spitfire's flaps, operated by compressed air, were either full up or full down, and the latter was close to 90 degrees of deflection. This was all drag and no lift, so there was no need to put them down until the field was made. *Robert Astrella*

One of the 7th Photo Group's hard-working PR.XIs rests on the ramp at Mount Farm, England, along with several other Spitfires, awaiting the next photo mission. The extra fuel added to the internal spaces of the airframe allowed a once short-ranged interceptor to stay airborne for up to seven hours. Operating in such cramped quarters at up to 40,000 feet and minus-60 degrees Fahrenheit for so long was extremely fatiguing to the pilots. *Robert Astrella*

missions. The low-altitude version (Merlin 66) was designated as the LF Mk VIII, while the high-altitude type (Merlin 70) was known as the HF Mk VIII. In all, Vickers-Supermarine built 1,658 Spitfire Mk VIIIs.

The extended-length, pointed tipped 40-foot, 2-inch wings, which had been engineered to help high-altitude stability, never worked well enough to benefit the fighter pilots who had to fly with them. Jeffrey Quill, who had many thousands of Spitfire flying hours, said: "From a pure flying point of view, the Mk VIII with the standard wingtips was the best. I hated the extended wingtips on the Mk VIII and did everything I could to get rid of them."

• • •

Spitfire Mk VIII Specifications

Wing span	36 feet, 10 inches (standard); 40 feet, 2 inches (extended)
Length	30 feet
Height	11 feet, 2 inches
Powerplant	1,580-horsepower Rolls-Royce Merlin 66 or 1,475-horsepower Merlin 70
Armament	"C" wing; four Hispano 20-mm cannons; could carry up to 1,000 pounds of bombs (one 250-pound bomb under either wing and one 500-pound bomb under the fuselage)
Maximum speed	400 miles per hour at 21,000 feet
Maximum range	1,200 miles on 1,200 gallons of fuel (internal and external tanks)
Rate of climb	2,850 feet per minute at sea level
Service ceiling	40,000 to 44,000 feet, depending on the time of endurance due to the lack of cockpit pressurization

• • •

This 14th Squadron, 7th Photo Group, Spitfire PR Mk XI at Mount Farm shows some of the unique characteristics of the Mark. The deepened lower cowling covers an enlarged oil tank for extended range; the one-piece windscreen without armor glass was a weight-saving measure. The recce boys weren't supposed to engage enemy fighters or ground defenses head-on, and the one-piece windscreen gave them better forward vision as well. *Robert Astrella*

Both sides spent a great deal of time analyzing captured aircraft, and the Spitfire was high on the list for the Luftwaffe. This Spitfire PR.XI was coded by the *Versuchsverband Oberkommando der Luftwaffe* as T9+EK for demonstration flying with *Sonderstaffel Wanderzirkus*. Both the Spitfire and the P-51 in the background are getting quite a bit of attention from line pilots who want a close-up look at their adversaries. *Eddie Creek via Alfred Price*

Spitfire Mk IX Series

Similar to the way the Spitfire Mk V series started out as re-engined Mk Is and Mk IIs, the Spitfire Mk IX series began life as re-engined Mk Vs. In all, Vickers-Supermarine manufactured a total of 5,665 of this series as low-, medium-, and high-altitude fighters, fighter-bombers, and fighter-interceptors. And these came equipped with the "B," "C," and "E" wing armament packages. The latter being armed with two Hispano 20-mm cannons (moved about 1 foot farther outboard) and two Browning .50-caliber machine guns. If required, the new Universal or "E" wing could also be configured with four instead of two Hispano 20-mm cannons and two .50-caliber machine guns. Obviously with the arrival of the "E" wing, the Spitfire's firepower had been improved dramatically.

During the Spitfire IX's production run, they appeared as follows: the F Mk IXB, F Mk IXC, and F Mk IXE for medium-altitude missions; the LF Mk IXB, LF Mk IXC, and LF Mk IXE for low-altitude operations; and the HF Mk IXB, HF Mk IXC, and the HF Mk IXE for high-altitude combat.

This Mk IX series of Spitfire fighters were powered by three main versions of the Rolls-Royce Merlin engine—the Merlin 61, 63, and 70, all using two-stage supercharger units.

Some Spitfire Mk IXs were ultimately fitted to carry the same 62-gallon external fuel drop tanks that were carried by North American P-51 Mustangs under their wings. This improvement, widely used and immensely popular among pilots, increased the Spitfire IX's total fuel capacity to 285 gallons. With its new speed, improved maneuverability, and longer range, the Mk IXs proved to be more than a match for Luftwaffe fighters. Still, neither Vickers-Supermarine nor the RAF were completely satisfied, and the development of the Spitfire breed went forth.

Spitfire F Mk IXC Specifications

Wing span	36 feet, 10 inches
Length	31 feet, 1/2 inch
Height	12 feet, 7 3/4 inches
Powerplant	1,565-horsepower Rolls-Royce Merlin 61 or 1,650-horsepower Merlin 63 with two-stage super-chargers
Armament	"C" wing, or four .303 machine guns and two 20-mm cannons
Maximum speed	410 miles per hour at 25,000 feet
Maximum range	980 miles on 175 gallons of fuel
Rate of climb	3,125 feet per minute at sea level
Service ceiling	42,500 feet

• • •

Spitfire PR Mk X: The Spitfire Mk IX series of fighters featured the high speed and the alterable altitude characteristics that RAF photo-recce units needed to perform their hazardous duties. This led to the production of the Spitfire PR Mk XI, but as an interim measure, the Spitfire PR Mk X appeared. These were powered by the 1,665-horsepower Merlin 77 engine. As they began to roll off their production line, the Mk IX fighter came about, and after only 16 examples of the PR Mk X had been built, production ended in favor of the Mk IX-based Spitfire PR Mk XI. In the end, though, the PR Mk Xs were inferior to most other photo-recce versions of the Spitfire, they remained in service until the war was over.

Spitfire PR Mk XI: Based upon the Mk IX series of fighters, the Spitfire PR Mk XI was a much improved photo-recce aircraft that was both fast and alterable in its duties. Depending on which powerplant it used, it could perform at all altitudes. Unarmed, the PR Mk XIs were at first powered by the 1,520-horsepower Rolls-Royce Merlin 61, or the 1,710-horsepower Merlin 63 or 63A engines. But later airframes were fitted with the 1,710-horsepower Merlin 70 engine. Vickers-Supermarine built 471 production PR Mk XIs.

As dedicated photographic reconnaissance and mapping platforms, the Spitfire PR Mk XI aircraft were equipped with vertical or oblique F8, F24, and F52 cameras with their varied focal lengths. Since they were an offshoot of the Mk IX fighter, their performance characteristics were the best of all Spitfire PR types. For example, when powered by the Merlin 70 engine, they had a maximum speed of 420 miles per hour at 26,500 feet, and their initial sea-level rate of climb was 4,000 feet per minute.

Spitfire Mk XII: The Spitfire Mk XII fighter began life much earlier than its designation indicates, as the Spitfire Mk IV fighter. This was the proposed Rolls-Royce Griffon-powered version, aborted because the Griffon engine was not available. In essence, the few Mk IVs that had been built served as prototypes to the Mk XIIs.

By late 1942, the Rolls-Royce Griffon engine was being manufactured in large enough numbers to supply Spitfire production. The first Spitfire Mk XII (DP485) appeared in October 1942, powered by a 1,735-horsepower Griffon III engine with a single-stage supercharger. Another 99 of these were built and powered by either the Griffon III or IV engines. As low-altitude fighter-interceptors, the Spitfire Mk XIIs first entered the war in the spring of 1943, with Nos. 41 and 91 Squadrons flying out of Hawkinge. Their first duty was to intercept F-W 190s that were raiding England's southern coast at tree-top level, in their attempt to get under Britain's extensive radar network.

For armament, the Spitfire Mk XIIs came equipped with the "B" wing, or four .303 machine guns and two 20-mm cannons. And, as the first production Spitfire to use the Griffon engine, their maximum speed was 393 miles per hour at 18,000 feet; they could reach 20,000 feet in 6.7 minutes.

As an aside, the 1,650-cubic-inch displacement series of Rolls-Royce Merlin engines became an instant success—especially for the Spitfire. Yet Rolls-Royce went farther still, to create the 2,240-cubic-inch Griffon engines, which likewise became legend. Still a V-type with 12 cylinders, the deeper and heavier Griffon engine featured larger-diameter pistons and cylinders and a longer throw for its connecting rods. But even though the Griffon had more girth and weight than its Merlin predecessor, its overall length had been reduced. Another difference was that the Griffon's rotation was reversed from the Merlin's counterclockwise (left-hand) to clockwise (right-hand), as viewed by a pilot. During the late 1950s and early 1960s, as much as 3,000 horsepower was wrung from the Griffon engines when they were powering American Unlimited Hydroplane race boats.

• • •

Spitfire Mk XII Specifications

Wing span	36 feet, 10 inches
Length	30 feet, 9 inches
Height	11 feet, 2 inches
Powerplant	1,735-horsepower Rolls-Royce Griffon III/IV with two-stage supercharger as they became available (single-stage early on)
Armament	"B" wing, or four Browning .303 machine guns and two Hispano 20-mm cannons
Maximum speed	393 miles per hour at 18,000 feet
Maximum range	400 miles on internal fuel
Rate of climb	4,000 feet per minute at sea level
Service ceiling	38,200 feet

• • •

Spitfire PR Mk XIII: The Spitfire PR Mk XIII was an armed, low-level version of the older Mk V series of fighters, powered by the 1,620-horsepower Rolls-Royce Merlin 32 engine. It carried only four .303 machine guns and for the most part used only a pair obliquely mounted F8 cameras for its photo-recce duties. Even though there were only 16 PR Mk XIIIs built and put into service, they had a very respectable top speed of 400 miles per hour and a healthy range of 700 miles with an under-belly external fuel tank. Still, with the concurrent appearance of the Spitfire PR Mk XIs, further Spitfire PR Mk XIII production was terminated.

Spitfire Mk XIV: From October 1943 and on, almost 1,000 (957 actual) Spitfire Mk XIV fighters were built. Early in 1943, Vickers-Supermarine converted six Spitfire Mk VIII airframes (JF316 to JF321) to accept the new 2,045-horsepower Rolls-Royce Griffon 65 engine with a two-stage supercharger. Other modifications included a five-bladed propeller, broad-chord vertical fin and rudder, and, more often than not, the improved visibility teardrop type of cockpit canopy with the cut-down aft fuselage. As the production Spitfire XIVs entered service, they were used either as low- or medium-altitude fighters, and were armed with the "C" or "E" wings.

The sixth Mk VIII airframe (JF321) was fitted with the 2,050-horsepower Griffon 85 engine and, to help eliminate the Griffon's immense torque, was equipped with two contra-rotating three-bladed propellers

Serving as Spitfire Mk XIV prototypes as it were, these half-dozen former Mk VIIIs entered flight-test with the pointed top vertical fin and rudder of broader chord for increased area and stability.

During production, three main versions of the Spitfire Mk XIV were manufactured: the Spitfire Mk XIVC, optimized for low- to medium-altitude operations; Spitfire LF XIVE, for low-altitude combat; and the Spitfire FR Mk XIVE, for armed photo-recce missions.

In addition to the Mk XIV's improved aerodynamics, which had been derived from their redesigned vertical tail, they also featured much stronger airframes to accommodate their heavier and more powerful Griffon engines. It should be noted that this was the first mass-produced version of the Spitfire to be powered by the awesome Griffon engine.

• • •

Spitfire Mk XIVC Specifications

Wing span	36 feet, 10 inches
Length	32 feet, 8 inches
Height	12 feet, 8 inches
Powerplant	2,050-horsepower Rolls-Royce Griffon 65 or 66 with two-stage supercharger
Armament	"C" wing or four Browning .303 machine guns and two Hispano 20-mm cannons
Maximum speed	420 miles per hour at 20,000 feet
Maximum range	450 on internal fuel
Rate of climb	4,580 feet per minute at sea level
Service ceiling	42,500-plus feet

• • •

Spitfire Mk XVI: The 1,054 Spitfire Mk XVI fighters were manufactured alongside the Spitfire Mk IXs. The Spitfire Mk XVIs were all but identical to the Spitfire Mk IXs with one exception. As it happened at the time, in the United States, the Packard Motor Company—once a highly respected builder of fairly expensive luxury-type automobiles, was manufacturing a low-altitude version of the Rolls-Royce Merlin 66 engine under license; it was designated as the Merlin 266. To distinguish the Packard Merlin 266-powered Spitfires from the Rolls-Royce Merlin 66-powered Spitfires, the Mk IXs were simply redesignated as Mk XVIs. As they were built alongside each other and featured the same armament and performance, the Spitfire Mk XVIs were merely Packard Merlin-powered Spitfire IXs.

Spitfire Mk XVIII: Following the production of nearly 1,000 Spitfire Mk XIV fighters, which had been completed by Vickers-Supermarine at its Castle Bromwich facility, a second generation of Rolls-Royce Griffon-powered Spitfires appeared. Fundamentally a definitive development of the Spitfire Mk XIV, the Spitfire Mk XVIII appeared in either the medium-altitude F Mk XVIII or the armed photo-recce FR Mk XVIII versions. Both versions came with the "E" wing (two cannons and two machine guns), but the FR Mk XVIII also carried three cameras. The F Mk XVIII (FR Mk 18 after the war) featured increased internal fuel capacity, with 66 gallons in the aft fuselage and 26 1/2 gallons in the wings. These Spitfires, powered by the Griffon 65 or 67 engines with two-stage superchargers, came with the rearview bubble-type cockpit canopy and had strengthened landing gear and wings. In total, there were 300 of these aircraft built—100 F Mk XVIIIs and 200 FR Mk XVIIIs.

• • •

Spitfire F Mk XVIII Specifications

Wing span	36 feet, 10 inches
Length	33 feet, 3 1/4 inches
Height	11 feet, 2 inches
Powerplant	2,375-horsepower Rolls-Royce Griffon 67 with two-stage supercharger (some with 2,050-horsepower Griffon 65)
Armament	"E" wing, or two Hispano 20-mm cannons and two Browning .50 machine guns
Maximum speed	442 miles per hour at 20,000 feet
Maximum range	800 miles on internal fuel
Rate of climb	5,000 feet per minute
Service ceiling	41,000 feet

• • •

Spitfire PR Mk XIX: The last photographic reconnaissance and mapping adaptation of the Spitfire line, the Spitfire PR Mk XIX, was not only the definitive photo-recce variant but the best photo-recce version of all. It also was the only unarmed rendition to be powered by the Rolls-Royce Griffon engine, the 2,050-horsepower Griffon 65 (the first 25) or 66 (the remaining 200). The Spitfire PR XIX prototype (SW777) and the first 24 production aircraft were completed without pressurized cockpits, while the remaining 200 had them; the last PR Mk XIX (PR Mk 19 after the war) came off the assembly line in early 1946. As a replacement for the older PR Mk XIs, the PR Mk XIXs were created from Mk XIV fighter airframes with strengthened Mk VC wings. The Spitfire PR XIXs boasted of a top speed of 460 miles per hour, a service ceiling of 43,000 feet, and a maximum range of 1,550 miles, with both internal and external fuel supplies. On 1 April 1954, a Spitfire PR Mk 19 (PS888) of No. 81 Squadron in Malaya made the Royal Air Force's final flight with an operational front-line Spitfire.

Spitfire F Mk 21: The Spitfire F Mk 21 fighter aircraft, which arrived too late to do battle in World War II, were the result of an extensive Spitfire redesign effort begun in 1944. The Spitfire F Mk 21 featured a new wing planform with increased area and a redesigned tail section. Gone was the Spitfire's elliptical wing planform, in favor of straighter leading edges and clipped tips.

To get the Spitfire F Mk 21 ball rolling, Vickers-Supermarine created a pair of prototypes, the Mk IV (DP485) and the fourth prototype Mk XIV (JF319). Both of these, the first Griffon-powered Spitfires, were designated Spitfire Mk XXs to avoid further confusion.

In any event, 122 Spitfire F Mk 21s were built, and they were powered by the 2,050-horsepower Griffon 61 or 65 engines with two-speed superchargers, turning five-bladed propellers. They were armed with four 20-mm cannons and could carry 1,000 pounds of either bombs or unguided rockets. This late model of the Spitfire first became operational with RAF No. 91 Squadron at West Malling, then No. 1 Squadron at Manston.

Spitfire F Mk 22: The Spitfire F Mk 22 prototype (PK312) and production aircraft featured the cut-down spine on the aft fuselage and the high-visibility bubble-type cockpit canopies.

The Germans went one step further in analyzing the Spitfire's capabilities by replacing the Merlin on this captured Mk VB (EN830) with a 1,475-horsepower Daimler-Benz DB 605A engine. With all armament removed and a weight of 6,000 pounds, the aircraft topped out at 379 miles per hour at 22,000 feet, compared to 385 miles per hour for an Me 109G with the same engine. *Alfred Price*

Other than these modifications, in addition to being powered by 2,045-horsepower Rolls-Royce Griffon 85 engines with two-stage superchargers, spinning two three-bladed propellers in opposite directions, the F Mk 22s were near carbon copies of the F Mk 21s. Some early production F Mk 22s were powered by Griffon 61 engines turning five-bladed propellers, but most of the 278 production F Mk 22s came with the Griffon 85s and the torque-reducing contra-rotating propeller system. These began to roll off the production line in March 1945, just prior to VE-Day, and therefore they did not see combat duties in the war.

Spitfire F Mk 23: Just one Spitfire F Mk 23 prototype was created from a Spitfire Mk VIII fighter (JG204), which featured a wing of a different cross-section for testing. The new wing's leading edge was raised upward approximately one inch to employ a laminar-flow type of wing, which had been engineered for incorporation on the Vickers-Supermarine Spiteful F Mk 14. In the end, the proposed Spitfire F Mk 23 did not enter into production, as it did not have enough improvement

over the Spitfire F Mk 22. Moreover, as it turned out during flight-test operations, the laminar-flow wing hindered rather than helped the Spitfire's already excellent handling qualities. This single Spitfire F Mk 23 served as the first of the Spiteful's three prototypes.

Spitfire F Mk 24: Now comes the last of the great Spitfire fighter breed, the Spitfire F Mk 24. These were manufactured with the increased-area vertical and horizontal tail assemblies, higher internal fuel capacity, four short-barrel Mk V Hispano 20-mm cannons, and underwing attachments for unguided aerial rockets, and they were powered by the Griffon 85 engines with contra-props. Only 54 Spitfire F Mk 24s were built and delivered, but another 22 were created from modified Spitfire F Mk 22s. The last production airplane (VN496) was delivered to RAF No. 80 Squadron in February 1948. With this action, finally after more than a decade of continuous production, the Spitfire's lengthy manufacturing process had ended.

Spitfire F Mark 22/24 Specifications

Wing span	36 feet, 11 inches
Length	32 feet, 8 inches
Height	12 feet, 8 inches
Powerplant	2,375-horsepower Rolls-Royce Griffon 85 with two-stage supercharger
Armament	Four long-barrel Mk II Hispano 20-mm cannons (F Mk 22) or four short-barrel Mk V Hispano 20-mm cannons (175 rounds per cannon inboard; 150 rounds per cannon outboard)
Maximum speed	450 miles per hour at 19,000 feet
Maximum range	580 to 945 miles, depending on the amount of fuel carried
Rate of climb	4,900 feet per minute at sea level
Service ceiling	43,000 feet

• • •

As the Spitfire F.21, F.22, and F.24 fighters, and the Seafire F Mk 46 and F Mk 47, appeared, it had become clear that the type had pretty much come to the end of its lineage.

After the war, as far as the Spitfire was concerned, the F.22 had been promoted to be the most significant type of piston-powered and propeller-driven fighter in service with the Royal Auxiliary Air Force during the 1946 to 1951 period, and some of these remained in service until 1953 with the Middle East Air Force.

In what became a desperate attempt to prolong production, though at the time it was a significant development, Vickers-Supermarine developed the epitome of the Spitfire—the Spiteful series of fighters, which began flight-test activities in June 1944, soon after D-Day.

The Vickers-Supermarine Spiteful Series

The Vickers-Supermarine Spiteful series of fighters were developed to supplement and ultimately replace the Spitfire series. Three variants—the Mk 14, Mk 15, Mk 16—were contracted for prototype form, but only the Mk 14 actually went into production.

The first of three Spiteful prototypes, the Mk 14, was formerly the one-of-kind Spitfire F Mk 23 prototype. Powered by the Griffon 65 engine and spinning a five-bladed propeller, the Mk 14 initiated its flight-test activities in June 1944. Although it and the Mk 15 and Mk 16 looked much like Spitfires, they shared an all-new design, with squared-off wings, wider-track inward-retracting landing gear (with doors), and so on. But due to the war's end and the arrival of the jet age, the Spiteful F Mk 14 program was terminated after the 17th airplane had been completed on 17 January 1947; the remaining 67-plane order was canceled.

The Spiteful F Mk 15 prototype was powered by either the Rolls-Royce Griffon 89 or 90, and had the contra-rotating three-bladed propellers. No production examples followed.

The prototype Spiteful F Mk 16 was powered by the Rolls-Royce Griffon 101 engine with a three-stage supercharger and awesome power. It hit a fantastic speed of 502 miles per hour in level-attitude flight during tests in early 1947. This was to no avail, however, as no production aircraft were built.

All of the Merlin- and Griffon-powered Spitfires were manufactured by the Supermarine Division of Vickers-Armstrongs Limited, with production facilities in Castle Bromwich, Southampton, Swindon, and Winchester, from 1938 to 1947. In all, 18,298 Merlin-powered and 2,053 Griffon-powered Spitfires were produced for a grand total of 20,351.

SEAFIRE SERIES:
MK IB THROUGH MK 47

The Seafire series of aircraft-carrier-based fighter aircraft was everything to the British Royal Navy that the Spitfire series of land-based fighters was to the British Royal Air Force. And except for their folding wingtips, beefed-up landing gear, colors and markings, and carrier arresting gear, they were navalized equals to their air force brothers. Indeed, because of their carrier arresting gear (cable grabbers), they were nicknamed the "hooked Spitfires."

The first Seafires were little more than Spitfire VBs with arresting hooks installed for deck trials and nicknamed "Hooked Spitfires." The first was BL676, seen during a test flight, converted by Air Service Training beginning in late 1941. The trials went so well that conversion was begun en masse to turn VBs into Seafire Mk IBs. *Alfred Price*

The hook on Mk VB BL687, another of the Air Service Training trial "Hooked Spitfires," was nothing short of substantial, mounted deep within the bulk of the fuselage. The excellent design and installation led pilots to say nothing drastic was needed, and Seafire conversion could begin right away. Hook failures on Seafires were rare. *Alfred Price*

In all, 2,408 Seafires were produced for the Royal Navy, either from converted Spitfires or as new-build aircraft. Of them, beginning with the first Seafire Mk IB (a modified Spitfire Mk VB), which was first flown in January 1942, there were eight distinct versions of the Seafire.

Seafire Mk IB: Since the Fleet Air Arm of the British Royal Navy was having good fortune with its Hawker Sea Hurricane fighters by mid-1941, and had realized just how good the Vickers-Supermarine Spitfires were doing for the Royal Air Force, the Royal Navy decided it was time to develop a navalized version of the Spitfire.

By late 1941, the first 48 conversions of Spitfire Mk VB aircraft to Seafire Mk IB aircraft had been accomplished at Hampshire by Air Service Training. These and an additional 118 "hooked Spitfires" were issued the designation Seafire IB; there were no new-build Seafire Mk IBs. The second of two Vickers-Supermarine subcontractors in Cunliffe-Owen at Eastleigh converted the remaining 118 Spitfire Mk VBs to Seafire Mk IBs, for a total of 166 aircraft, without folding wingtips.

• • •

Seafire Mk IB Specifications

Wing span	36 feet, 10 inches
Length	29 feet, 11 inches
Height	10 feet, 1 inch
Powerplant	1,440-horsepower Rolls-Royce Merlin Mk 45 with a two-stage supercharger (some were powered by the identically rated tropicalized Merlin Mk 46)
Armament	Two Hispano 20-mm cannons and four Browning .303 machine guns
Maximum speed	370 miles per hour
Maximum range	470 miles (85 gallons internal fuel)
Rate of climb	2,660 feet per minute at sea level
Service ceiling	36,700 feet

• • •

Since the Seafire Mk IB fighter was essentially a Spitfire Mk VB with the mixed armament

A flight deck full of Seafire IIIs aboard the HMS *Slinger* at Brisbane, Australia, in August 1945, are on the way to replenish British carriers off Japan, just before the end of the war. The national marking roundels had the American-style bars added as an aid for friendly gunners and fighter pilots who might not have been used to seeing the elliptical wing shape in the sky. Anything strange was fair game to most on the prowl for enemy aircraft. *Scales via Alfred Price*

"B" wing, two cannons and four machine guns, it was powered by the same types of Rolls-Royce Merlin engines (Mk 45 or 46) with near-equal performance characteristics. However, as converted rather than optimized fighters, the initial batch of 166 Seafire Mk IBs were looked upon as

Basically a seaborne version of the RAF Mk V, the Seafire Mk III was the first Royal Navy example with folding wings, and the first to be mass-produced. The Seafire was well-loved by carrier pilots, who thought it both excellent in the air and easy to bring aboard ship at low speed. The single major complaint, as with most versions of the aircraft, was lack of range. Carrier pilots had to plan their sorties very carefully if they were doing much more than intercepting enemy aircraft trying to attack the fleet. *National Archives*

interim aircraft. And though they were successful, the Royal Navy demanded its own new production type. Thus, the Seafire Mk IIC was born.

Seafire Mk IIC: As the first true production version of the Seafire, the Mk IIC variant was the Royal Navy's version of the RAF's Spitfire Mk VC. It was powered by either the Rolls-Royce Merlin 45 or 46 engine, although a few had the Merlin 32. The Seafire Mk IIC featured the Spitfire-developed "universal" or "C" wing armament system, with either eight .303 machine guns or two 20-mm cannons and four machine guns.

For its production program, both Vickers-Supermarine and Westland manufactured a total of 262 Seafire Mk IICs, and on 15 June 1942, the Fleet Air Arm of the Royal Navy accepted its first combat-ready example.

The Rolls-Royce Merlin Mk 32-powered version of the Seafire Mk IIC, optimized for low-alti-

A Seafire Mk III carries two 200-pound smoke floats under each wing, as well as a belly tank for extended range, something often needed at sea. The Mk III, the first definitive shipborne Seafire, was the first to incorporate folding wings, a necessity to get a full air wing aboard. The Seafire retained all the best qualities of the Spitfire, becoming a significant addition to the Royal Navy's combat capability. *Alfred Price*

A Seafire XV from 803 Squadron, Royal Canadian Navy, taxies across the wires on HMCS *Warrior* in 1946. Unlike most Griffon-powered Spitfires and Seafires, these RCN XVs were fitted with a four-bladed propeller instead of a five-bladed one. The water on deck, combined with oil and fuel, made traction tenuous. Even very little power could move a fighter with fully locked brakes down the deck. *Public Archives of Canada via Alfred Price*

No. 803 Squadron, Royal Canadian Navy, Seafire Mk XVs in operation off the HMCS *Warrior* in 1946. The XV was the first Griffon-powered Seafire and the only one to enter service before World War II ended, though four more Griffon Seafire variants followed. Even with no wind across the deck, a Seafire could get airborne in a very short distance. The warning RAF pilots were given about half power on the Griffon until airborne held especially true for carrier pilots. *Public Archives of Canada via Alfred Price*

tude combat situations, was known as the Seafire L Mk IIC variant. Another subvariant, the Seafire PR Mk IIC, was powered like the former but served as an armed (four machine guns) low- to medium-altitude photographic reconnaissance aircraft. Having but one oblique F24 camera mounted within its aft fuselage section, it was the equivalent of the RAF's Spitfire PR Mk XIII.

Seafire Mk III: The Seafire Mk III was the first to be manufactured with folding wingtips to reduce their parking areas aboard carriers. With the exception of this feature and the Mk III's use of the Rolls-Royce Merlin 55M engine, it was essentially a Mk IIC, a medium-altitude fighter.

One sub-version, the Seafire L Mk III, was powered by the Merlin 55M engine, which was optimized for low-altitude missions. Another subvariant, the Seafire PR Mk III, was specifically used for photographic reconnaissance missions and was outfitted with two F24 cameras in the aft fuselage.

In total, 1,220 Seafire Mk III aircraft of all versions were produced by Vickers-Supermarine

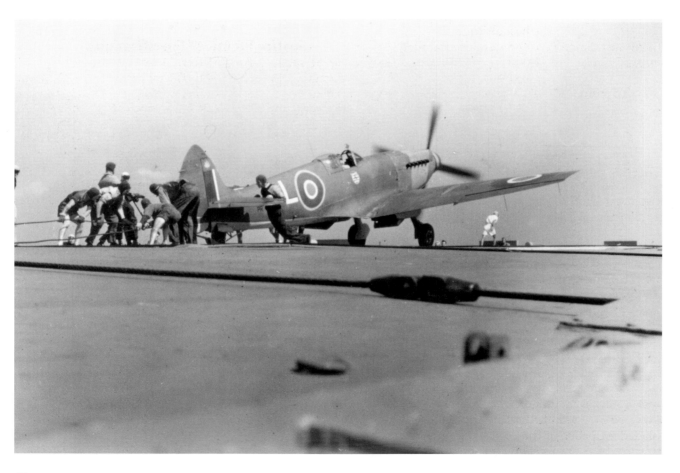

and subcontractors Cunliffe-Owen and West-land, making this variant the first mass-produced version of the Seafire.

Seafire Mk XV: Since it was the first version of the Seafire to be powered by the awesome Rolls-Royce Griffon engine—specifically, the 1,750-horsepower Griffon Mk VI—the Seafire Mk XV was a much improved warplane. The Mk XV boasted a rate of climb in excess of 4,000 feet per minute and a top speed of more than 400 miles per hour. The 390 Seafire Mk XV fighters were the only wartime Seafires to be powered by the Griffon engine.

• • •

Seafire Mk XV Specifications

Wing span	36 feet, 10 inches
Length	32 feet, 3 inches
Height	12 feet, 9 inches
Powerplant	1,750-horsepower Rolls-Royce Griffon Mk VI with a single-stage supercharger
Armament	Universal "C" wing
Maximum speed	400-plus miles per hour at best altitude
Maximum range	400 miles (internal fuel)
Rate of climb	4,000 feet per minute at sea level
Service ceiling	37,500 feet

• • •

Seafire Mk XVIII: The Seafire Mk XVII, or Mk 17, of which 232 examples were built, was very similar to the Seafire Mk XV aircraft but with two major differences: strengthened landing gear and a cut-down aft fuselage (dorsal spine) with a bubble-type cockpit canopy.

An undocumented number of these were completed at the factory as photographic reconnaissance aircraft, designated Seafire PR Mk XVII. They carried a pair of F24 cameras in the aft fuselage section.

These Rolls-Royce Griffon Mk VI-powered Seafires came on line too late to see combat duty in World War II, but served until the mid-1950s.

Seafire Mk 45: For all intent, the Seafire Mk 45 was a navalized version of the Spitfire Mk 21. Powered by either the Griffon 61 spinning a five-bladed propeller, or the Griffon 85 turning a pair of three-bladed propellers in opposite directions,

the Seafire Mk 45 was capable of nearly 450 miles per hour. But as the war was ending, only 50 of these marvelous fighters were built.

Seafire Mk 46: The Seafire Mk 46, of which only 24 examples were produced, featured the improvements enjoyed by the Spitfire Mk 22. But, it was soon realized, these improvements were not sufficient to warrant further production. Most of the Seafire Mk 46 fighter planes were converted to dedicated photographic reconnaissance aircraft and redesignated FR Mk 46s.

Seafire FR Mk 47: Manufactured from the outset to perform photographic reconnaissance duties, the Seafire FR Mk 47 was powered by either the Griffon 87 or 88 engines, turning a pair of contra-rotating three-bladed propellers. As a photo-recce plane, the FR Mk 47 carried two electrically heated F24 cameras in the aft fuselage section.

In total, Vickers-Supermarine produced 140 Seafire FR Mk 47 aircraft. The last of these rolled off its production line in March 1949, to end more than 10 full years of constant Spitfire and Seafire manufacture.

• • •

Seafire FR Mk 47 Specifications

Wing span	36 feet, 11 inches
Length	34 feet, 4 inches
Height	12 feet, 9 inches
Powerplant	2,350-horsepower Rolls-Royce Griffon 87 or 2,375-horsepower Griffon 88 with two-stage superchargers
Armament	Four Hispano Mk V 20-mm cannons; one 250-pound or one 500-pound general-purpose bomb under either wing; or eight unguided high-explosive rockets under either wing
Maximum speed	452 miles per hour at 20,000 feet
Maximum range	1,475 miles with addition of external fuel tanks
Rate of climb	4,800 feet per minute at sea level
Service ceiling	38,250 feet

• • •

Being carrier-based, Royal Navy Seafires were deployed over the world's oceans. Although they were produced in a much smaller number than Spitfires, the Seafires accounted themselves well, especially against the Germans in the North Sea, the Italians in the Mediterranean Sea, and the Japanese in the Pacific Ocean.

In total, Vickers-Supermarine manufactured 2,408 Seafires for the Royal Navy, including 166 from converted Spitfire Mk VBs and 2,242 new-build airplanes derived from various Spitfire types.

As with the Spitfire, Vickers-Supermarine continued to further develop its Seafire, and in mid-1944 unveiled the Seafang series of carrier-based fighters.

The Seafang

In the very same way the Spiteful series of RAF fighters was to supplement and ultimately replace the Spitfire, so was the Seafang destined to reinforce and finally displace the Seafire.

During the late stages of World War II, the Royal Navy ordered two types of the Seafang: the Mk 31 and the Mk 32. The former was powered by the Rolls-Royce Griffon 61, and the latter by the Griffon 89. As many as 150 Seafangs of both types had been ordered before the program was terminated in early 1947, but only eight Mk 31s and ten Mk 32s were completed.

The rapidly encroaching jet age put a halt on the development of piston-powered and pro-

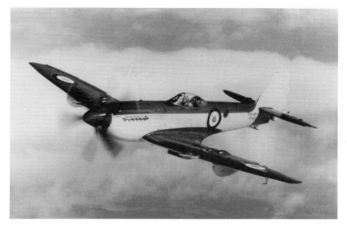

The very last of the line, the Seafire FR Mk 47, which bore little resemblance to the early short-nosed Spitfire. Two contra-rotating propellers came as standard issue on this fighter. Fitted with guns and cameras, it gave carrier commanders a flexibility that was well used when the FR.47 went to war in Korea. The last of 140 FR.47s was pushed out in March 1949. *Alfred Price*

A study in power . . . the Seafire 45, basically a navalized version of the Spitfire 21. Due to the approaching end of World War II, only 50 were built, but they could really scream, at around 450 miles per hour. The large fairing doors were part of the reason for the increased speed, preventing excessive drag in the wheelwells. Some were fitted with twin three-bladed contra-rotating propellers to neutralize the massive Griffon's torque, an elegant solution that worked quite well. *Alfred Price*

peller-driven fighters like the Spiteful and Seafang, although both featured unheard-of performance.

One Spiteful F Mk 16 with a 2,375-horsepower Griffon 101 engine reached an incredible 494 miles per hour at an altitude of 22,500 feet in level-attitude flight. And a Seafang F Mk 32 with a 2,350-horsepower Griffon 89 hit 475 miles per hour at 21,350 feet in level flight. As outstanding as these performance marks were for propeller-driven aircraft, they pale when compared to the 600-plus-miles-per-hour speeds then being flown

on a daily basis by turbojet-powered fighter aircraft. And it was not long before a four-jet commercial airliner, the de Havilland Comet, exceeded 500 miles per hour!

The Spitfire and the Seafire were both among the very best of the World War II fighter aircraft. Yet with the emergence of the Spiteful and Seafang, it is obvious that if the war had continued beyond September 1945, Great Britain would have had a pair of new fighters that were more than adequate replacements to the Spitfire and Seafire.

THE SPITFIRE DESCRIBED

Most of us have heard the phrase, "She's a real spitfire!" But where this phrase actually came from remains a mystery. A spitfire is described as a person who is easily aroused to violent outbursts of anger. Our Spitfire fighter plane truly was an easily excitable lady that performed furious eruptions of rage. Still her designer, R. J. Mitchell, did not really care much for the name she was given. Though in the end, after she had proved her worth to her kingdom, the name Spitfire turned out to be more than appropriate.

When the Mitchell-designed Vickers-Supermarine Type 300 prototype appeared in its original

The classic lines of the early short-nosed Spitfire Marks remained basically unchanged through the Mk V. This Spit V flew from Eastleigh for the first time on 23 April 1941 and was then transferred to The U.S. Army Air Corps for evaluation in America. This shot of the aircraft was taken at Wright Field, Ohio, the service test facility, on 29 July 1941, many months before the U.S. entered World War II. As with most Americans, the test pilots at Wright found the aircraft viceless and great fun to fly, though all commented on the lack of range. *USAF*

The prototype tropicalized Spitfire VB, fitted with the massive Vokes air filter, was a disappointment since performance, already marginal, was lowered even more. Unfortunately, there was no other way to protect the Merlin from eating sand and dust. The 90-gallon belly tank was attached to ferry the aircraft to Malta for combat testing—an excellent choice since the tiny island was being hammered mercilessly by the Luftwaffe. *RAF via Alfred Price*

form in early 1936, it was a far cry from the Spitfire versions it ultimately spawned. When it made its first public showing in mid-1936, few other fighter-type aircraft in the world could challenge her speed, agility, maneuverability, and looks. She was to be a winner, and everyone knew it—especially the British Air Ministry, which had placed an order for 310 examples, even before the Type 300 had been

fully evaluated by either its manufacturer or the RAF. And except for the 600 Hawker Hurricanes already on order, this was the largest first order ever awarded for a new plane in Great Britain.

When the original baby-blue Type 300 proto-type first took wing on 5 March 1936, the brand-new Spitfire's friendly and not-so-friendly rival fighters were:

An "erk" carefully polishes the canopy of a No. 122 Squadron Spit V. Long before other nations caught on to the benefits, Supermarine fitted a bulged bubble-style canopy to the Spitfire, enabling the pilot to actually lean over the cockpit sill and look rearward. In combination with the mirror on the windscreen canopy bow, this was an enormous leap forward in keeping sight of enemy aircraft, usually an important factor in winning a dogfight. *Alfred Price*

1. The American-made Seversky P-35. A single-seat, single-engine monoplane powered by the Pratt & Whitney Wasp series of R-1830 radial engines. It was armed with two engine cowl-mounted and two wing-mounted machine guns, and had a top speed of about 280 miles per hour.

2. The American-made Curtiss P-36 Hawk. A single-seat, single-engine monoplane powered by the Pratt & Whitney Wasp series of R-1830 radial engines. It was armed with two engine cowl-mounted and two wing-mounted machine guns, and had a top speed of about 310 miles per hour.

3. The German Messerschmitt Me 109. A single-seat, single-engine monoplane powered by the Daimler-Benz DB 601 series of inline engines. It was armed with two 7.92-mm machine guns and one 15-mm cannon, and had a top speed of about 290 miles per hour.

4. The German-made Focke-Wulf F-W 190. A single-seat, single-engine monoplane powered by the BMW 801 series of radial engines. It was armed with two to four 20-mm cannons and two 13-mm engine cowl guns, and had a top speed of about 420 miles per hour.

5. The Japanese-made Mitsubishi A6M Reisen (Zero fighter). A single-seat, single-engine monoplane powered by the Nakajima NK1 Sakae series of radial engines. It was armed with two 7.7-mm machine guns and two 20-mm cannons, and had a top speed of about 330 miles per hour.

6. The Russian-made Yakovlev Yak-9. A single-seat, single-engine monoplane powered by the VK-105PF-1/-3 series of inline engines. It was armed with one 12.7-mm cannon and one 20-mm cannon, and had a top speed of about 340 miles per hour.

7. The French-made Dewoitine 520. A single-seat, single-engine monoplane powered by the Hispano-Suiza 12Y45 series of inline engines. It was armed with four 7.5-mm machine guns and one 20-mm cannon, and had a top speed of about 330 miles per hour.

8. The French-made Morane-Saulnier MS 406. A single-seat, single-engine monoplane powered by the Hispano-Suiza 12Y31 series of inline engines. It was armed with four 7.5 mm machine guns and one 20 mm cannon, and had a top speed of about 300 miles per hour.

9. The British-made Hawker Hurricane Mk I. A single-seat, single-engine monoplane powered by the Rolls-Royce Merlin series of inline engines. It was armed with eight .303 machine guns, and had a top speed of about 325 miles per hour.

While most of the above countries had more improved fighters under development, it was to be a very long time before any of them could match or exceed the Spitfire's performance levels.

The Spitfire series, excluding the small number of Tr.8 and Tr.9 dual-seat trainers, were all single-seat, single-engine, low-wing monoplanes that were used as low-, medium-, and high-altitude fighters, fighter-bombers, fighter-interceptors, and as both armed and unarmed photographic reconnaissance and mapping aircraft. They were powered by a series of inline V-12 engines that were manufactured by Rolls-Royce in England and the Packard Motor Company in America. These supercharger-equipped V-type engines were affectionately named Merlin for the small, dark falcon—not the magician who helped King Arthur, and Griffon for the mythical half-lion, half-eagle monster. They offered from 990 to 2,375 horsepower and spun two-, three-, four-, five-, and even six-bladed propellers.

The Spitfire's fuel supply was at first carried in two tanks, which totaled 85 gallons, that were mounted one above the other just forward of the cockpit. The plane's fuel capacity continued to increase with the adoption of internal wing tanks, aft fuselage tanks, and external tanks.

Wing armament (there were never any cannons or guns mounted anywhere else on the Spitfires) was varied: (1.) four Browning .303 machine guns (the "A" wing); (2.) eight Browning .303 machine guns (the "B" wing); (3.) four Browning .303 machine guns and two Hispano Mk II 20-mm cannons (the "C" wing); (4.) Two Browning .50 machine guns and two Hispano Mk II 20-mm cannons (the "E" wing); and (5.) two Hispano Mk II (long-barrel) and two Hispano Mk V (short-bar-

Armorers clean and re-arm the 20-mm cannon on a No. 122 Squadron Mark V. Though cannons were fitted to earlier versions to test their feasibility, it was this Mark that had them installed as standard issue. The results were quite dramatic, upping the fighter's lethal capability significantly. Purists like Douglas Bader did not want to give up the eight .303s, but most came around once they got used to it. *Alfred Price*

The feasibility of installing four 20-mm cannons was tested on several Mark Vs, like this VC, and though this did not become standard for some time, the results were excellent, eventually leading to the later versions coming so equipped. The development of the "C" wing made such installations easy, since the structure was designed to take a good mixture of cannon and machine guns. *RAF via Alfred Price*

To enhance handling and increase roll rate, many Spitfires, like this LF Mark IX, came with their wings clipped, quite a simple thing to do since the tips were easily removed or installed. This aircraft also has attach points under the wings for four air-to-ground rockets, making it quite a lethal low-level fighter. The only drawback to the Spitfire for ground-attack work was a that a hit in the radiators or coolant lines would bring it down in a matter of minutes. *RAF via Alfred Price*

rel) 20-mm cannons. Moreover, a "Universal Wing" could carry different combinations of armament. For ground attack, Spitfires could carry up to 1,000 pounds of bombs (usually one 250-pound bomb under either wing and a 500-pound bomb under the fuselage) and up to 10 unguided high-explosive rockets. The photographic reconnaissance and mapping versions of the Spitfire carried several different cameras with special focal lengths for their low-, medium-, and high-altitude operations. These were mounted in the wings and aft fuselage areas of the photo-recce Spits and shot both vertical (straight down) and oblique (off to either side) photographs for the intelligence corps.

An engine-driven hydraulic fluid pump supplied the power for the Spitfire's landing-gear retraction and extension operations, while an air compressor allowed for the pneumatic execution of the wing flaps, wheel brakes, cannons, and machine guns.

With the Spitfire VII came a vast leap in medium- and high-altitude performance. The cockpits on many were pressurized, so the canopy had to be bolted on, while the wingtips were extended and the tailwheel retracted to enhance high-altitude capability. This pressurized F.VIIC, EN474, still exists and is on display at the National Air and Space Museum, Smithsonian Institution, Washington, DC. *NASM*

A very special Mk IXC, MK210, waits on the ramp at Wright Field, Ohio, on 13 May 1944. The fighter was transferred to the USAAF for range extension modification, resulting in the addition of a 43-gallon rear fuselage tank, 16.5-gallon flexible wing leading-edge tanks, and fittings for 62-gallon drop tanks, for a total of 285 gallons. Unfortunately, according to USAAF test pilot Gus Lundquist, it turned the delightful Spitfire into a real dog until most of the fuel was burned off. That summer Lundquist flew the fighter across the Atlantic to the RAF test facility at Boscombe Down, where the English pilots thoroughly agreed with Lundquist's assessment. *USAF*

Although a few of the later models did not have true elliptical planform flying surfaces, the Spitfire's wings and tailplanes are elliptical in planform and suited the aircraft very well indeed. The wing flaps are of the split-type and had but two positions—up (fully retracted) and down (fully extended). Because of this, they could not be used to assist take off maneuvers. The Spitfire's vertical stabilizer and rudder, and its horizontal stabilizer and elevators, are of a then-common variety with numerous bellcranks and cables. And of course, as with the ailerons, the rudder and elevators have spring-loaded trim tabs. Coauthor Jeff Ethell added: "Its overall flying qualities are terrific. It is a pleasure to fly, and as proved by history, its air-to-air combat maneuvers were crisp and decisive."

The Spitfire—from the Mk I of 1938 to the Mk 24 of 1948—was stable about all three axes, pitch, roll, and yaw. And beginning with the Spitfire Mk IIA and Mk IIB, when metal-covered ailerons had replaced the Mk I's fabric-covered ones, lateral (sideways) control became much lighter, and the pilots who were now familiar with the improved lateral control had to be careful not to overstress the wings during high G maneuvers. Equal care had to be reserved in the use of the metal-covered elevators, which were very light and sensitive.

The Spitfire had sensitive elevators, and if the spade-type flight control stick (column) was yanked back too quickly in maneuvers, such as in a loop or a steep turn, a high-speed stall would occur. When that came about, there was a violent shudder and clattering noise throughout the airframe, which tended to flip it over to one side or the other, and unless the control stick was pushed forward instantly, a rigid roll and spin would ensue.

Spinning was only allowed by Spitfire pilots who had written permission from the commanding officer of their squadron. The loss of altitude involved in a spin recovery maneuver was generally very great, and the following altitude limits

At Brno in 1946, Czech 7 Air Regiment (IV) clipped-wing Spitfire LF.IXs wait for inspection. Many foreign nations received multiple Marks of the Spitfire, finding their life far extended beyond World War II. Many of the fighters in this shot were sold to Israel in the late 1940s to make up a significant part of the IAF's early equipment. *Zdenek Hurt via Alfred Price*

were strictly enforced: Spins were not be started below 10,000 feet; recovery must be initiated no lower than 5,000 feet; and a speed of more than 150 miles per hour should be attained before starting to ease out of the resulting dive.

The Spitfire was exceptionally good for aerobatics. But because of its high performance and sensitive aileron, elevator, and rudder controls, care had to be taken not to impose excessive loads either on the plane itself or the pilot, and to avoid a high-speed stall. The following speeds were recommended for aerobatics:

1. Looping speed had to be about 300 miles per hour, but could be reduced to 220–250 miles per hour, if the pilot was fully proficient.
2. Rolling speed had to be anywhere between 180 and 300 miles per hour. The nose should be brought up about 30 degrees above the horizon at the start, the roll being barreled just enough to keep the engine running throughout.
3. Half roll-off loop speed had to be 320–350 miles per hour.
4. Upward roll speed had to be about 350–400 miles per hour.
5. Flick maneuvers (hard loops and rolls) were not permitted.

As the war progressed, and newer and better versions of the Spitfire appeared, many upcoming RAF Spitfire combat pilots first acquainted themselves with the aircraft in the form of the Mk IIA or Mk IIB fighters. This is part of what they found:

Primary Systems

The Vickers-Supermarine Spitfire Mk IIA and Spitfire Mk IIB fighters came powered by the 1,175-horsepower Rolls-Royce Merlin XII engine, spinning either a de Havilland 20-degree or Rotol 35-degree pitch constant-speed propeller. The

Ground crew re-arm the 20-mm Hispano cannon on this No. 303 (Polish) Squadron Mark IX. The reason for the bump on top of all cannon-equipped Spitfires is clear here—the ammo belt feed drum could not fit into the wing without this quick and simple modification. The drum's preloaded spring rewound with every recoil of the gun and removed the rounds from the belt before feeding them into the breech. The fuel cap has been removed from the fuselage tank at the bottom of the photo, indicating the aircraft is being refueled as well—standard operating procedure, since the Spitfire needed all the fuel it could get under most circumstances. *Alfred Price*

main difference was in their armament of eight .303 machine guns (Mk IA) and four .303 guns and two 20-mm cannons (Mk IIB).

The fuel was carried in two tanks mounted one above the other, the top tank holding 48 gallons and the lower one 37 gallons, for a total of 85 gallons. The lower tank was self-sealing forward of the cockpit, with the top tank feeding into the lower tank.

The Merlin XII's oil was supplied by a tank that held 5.8 gallons. It was fitted below the engine mounts, and the oil was cooled by a pair of oil coolers that were mounted in tandem and fitted to the bottom of the left (port) wing.

An engine-driven hydraulic fluid pump supplied the hydraulic power for the landing-gear operations, and an engine-driven air compressor fed two air storage cylinders for operating brakes,

flaps, machine guns/cannons, and landing lights. The air cylinders were connected in series, and each one held air at 200 pounds per square inch.

A 12-volt generator, controlled by a switch above the instrument panel, supplied an accumulator, which in turn supplied the whole of the electrical system. A voltmeter was on the left side of the switch.

Basic Flying Controls

The control column was of the spade-grip style and incorporated the machine gun and cannon firing mechanisms and the wheel brake lever. The rudder pedals had two positions for the feet and were adjustable for leg reach by rotating star-type adjustment knobs on sliding tubes aft of the rudder pedals.

The flying controls locking devices were

Several Spitfires, including several Mk Vs and this Mk IX, were modified as float-plane fighters for possible operations against German transport aircraft from secret camouflaged bases in the Balkans. Events overtook the need, and the project was dropped. Even though the largest propeller fitted to a Spitfire (11 feet, 3 inches) could absorb more engine power, the 25-foot, 7-inch floats and associated modifications slowed the fighter down by 45 miles per hour, and the rate of climb deteriorated by 20 percent. *NASM*

A No. 16 Squadron PR.XI is prepped for a sortie in the fall of 1944. One of the cameras is on the ground, ready for installation, and the pilot's parachute rests under the left wing. The PR Spitfires were quite easy to service, as the camera mounts were based on quick disconnects with rails, upon which the magazines and lenses could be run in and out of the aircraft. *Alfred Price*

A very clean No. 541 Squadron PR.XI flies across a cloud deck in June 1944, when the unit was very active in photographing the Normandy breakout and subsequent push into France. The PRU Blue camouflage was quite effective at high altitude, where it blended into the haze—the black-and-white invasion stripes had the perfect effect of destroying that camouflage. Allied planners considered it more important to tell their anti-aircraft gunners not to shoot at friendly aircraft than let the aircraft hide from enemy fighters. *Alfred Price*

stowed on the right (starboard) side of the cockpit behind the seat. To lock the control column, the longer device should be clamped to the control column handle at one end and the other end inserted in a key-hole slot in the right side of the seat. The fixed pin on the free end of the arm attached to this strut at the control column end should then be inserted in a lug on the starboard datum longeron, forming a rigid triangle between the column, the seat, and the longeron.

To lock the rudder pedals, a short bar with a pin at each end was attached to the other struts by a cable. The longer of the two pins should be inserted in a hole in the starboard star wheel bearing, and the shorter in an eyebolt on the fuselage frame directly below the front edge of the seat. The controls should be locked with the seat in its highest position.

Flying Instruments

A standard blind-flying instrument panel was incorporated in the main panel. The instruments were an airspeed indicator, altimeter, directional gyro, artificial horizon, rate-of-climb and descent indicator, and turn and bank indicator.

Trim Tabs

The elevator trimming tabs were controlled by a hand wheel on the left side of the cockpit, the indicator being on the instrument panel. The rudder trimming tab was controlled by a small hand wheel and did not have an indicator. The Mk IIA and Mk IIB fighters tended to turn to starboard when the hand wheel was rotated clockwise.

Landing Gear

The landing-gear selector lever moved in a gated quadrant, on the right side of the cockpit.

The prototype PR Mk XIII was developed for low-level reconnaissance; this PR Mk XIII differed from a PR.VII only in the fittings for drop tanks. Few PR.XIIIs were produced as such; most were simply converted from VIIs. *RAF via Alfred Price*

An automatic cut-out in the control moved the selector lever into the gate when it was pushed or pulled to the full extent of the quadrant.

To raise the outward retracting landing gear, the lever was pushed forward, but it first had to be pulled aftward then across to disengage it from the gate. When the landing gear was raised and locked, the lever would spring into the forward gate.

To lower the landing gear, the lever was pulled back, but it had to be pushed forward and then across to disengage it from the gate. When the landing gear was down and locked, the lever would spring back into the rear gate.

The electrically operated visual indicator featured two transparent windows on which the words UP on a red background and DOWN on a green background are lettered. These words were only visible according to the position of the landing gear. The switch for the DOWN circuit of the indicator was mounted on the inboard side of the throttle quadrant and was moved to the ON position by means of a striker on the throttle lever. This switch should be returned to the OFF position by hand when the airplane was left unattended for any length of time. The UP circuit was not controlled by this switch.

A metal rod that extended through the top surface of the wing was fitted to each main landing gear unit. When the gear was down, the rods protruded through the top of the wings, and when the gear was up, the top of the rods, which were painted red, were flush with the wing's upper surface.

A push-button switch controlled the warning horn and was mounted on the throttle quadrant and was operated by a striker on the throttle lever. The horn could be silenced, even though the landing gear wheels were retracted and the engine throttled back, by depressing the push button on the side of the throttle quadrant. As soon as the throttle was again advanced beyond about one quarter of its travel, the push button was automatically released and the horn would sound again on its return.

As for emergency operation of the landing gear, a sealed high-pressure cylinder containing carbon dioxide and connected to the landing-gear operating jacks was provided for use in the event of failure of the hydraulic system. The cylinder was mounted on the right side of the cockpit, and the seal could be punctured by means of a red-painted lever beside it. The handle was marked EMERGENCY ONLY, and provision was made for fitting a thin copper wire seal as insurance against inadvertent use.

PHOTO GALLERY

The ground crew straps their pilot into his No. 222 Squadron Spitfire VB for a sortie on 4 May 1942. Numerically, the Mark V was the most important version of the Spitfire, though it was outclassed by its contemporaries, the Me 109G and the F-W 190A. At this point in the war, most Spitfire sorties were low-level fighter sweeps across the Channel to the continent. *RAF Museum*

The "Flying Scotsman" of No. 222 Squadron gets a bit of a stack fire from overpriming his Spit VB, on 4 May 1942. The difference between underpriming or overpriming a Merlin was only about a thimbleful of fuel. When the engine was cold, it usually took four to six strokes on the massive Kigas plunger; when it was warm, even a partial stroke could yield these results. *RAF Museum*

A Spit VB, already well-worn by July 1942, gets serviced. The workhorse of the post-Battle of Britain period, the Mark V held the fort against the opposition until the improved Mk IX, meant to be nothing more than a stopgap, arrived on the scene. Once the improved Merlin engines, with increased supercharging, were installed, the Spitfire took on new life as a world-class fighter. *J. P. Crowder via Dorothy Helen Crowder*

As newer Spitfires began to come on line, the older Marks were slated for secondary jobs, if they weren't completely clapped out. Usually they were turned over to operational transition units (OTUs) to give newly graduated pilots a taste of flying fighters. This old Mark V has certainly seen better days, but is still enabling pilots to learn what it takes to fly a Spitfire. *Stan Walsh*

When the Seafire arrived for service with the Royal Navy, carrier pilots were eager to get it into combat. The sparkling characteristics remained, and the fighter was an immediate favorite. These two Seafire Mk IICs escort a Sea Hurricane on a practice sortie out of Yeovilton on 18 November 1942. Both types made excellent carrier-borne fighters, filling a gap until purpose-built naval fighters could come on line. *RAF Museum*

A training flight of old Mark IAs heads across England in the late afternoon sun of 18 November 1942. Even though the Mark I was obsolete, it was still being built through September 1942, to fill gaps in the OTUs spread across the UK. At that point in the war, Britain was still almost alone, and much in need of every airframe possible. *RAF Museum*

Several Mark IXs sit on the line in England in late 1944. The invasion stripes on the bottom of the fuselage are just visible, a holdover from June 1944, when they were painted across the top and bottom of the fuselage and wings. By 1945 they were removed entirely, as Allied gunners became less edgy. *A. C. Sloan*

Many nationalities flew Spitfires during the war, often forming their own squadrons within the RAF, and the Free French were no exception. This Mark IX was attached to one of the French squadrons on the continent in 1945. Pilots from nations that had been overrun by the Germans were often so fierce in their determination to engage the enemy that they would wade into situations where they were greatly outnumbered. *via Tom Hitchcock*

The weather in Italy was either sunny or rainy, and that was fine until fighters had to be flown out of swirling dust or tire-sucking mud. Pierced steel plank, like this piece a Spitfire IX is traversing in Italy late in 1944, solved the problem of sinking into the mud, but the surface was so slimy there was virtually no directional control on landing. *James Stitt*

"Sitzmark 1" was 31st Fighter Group pilot Bill Skinner's first Spitfire Mk VIII. Considered by many pilots, including Jeffrey Quill, the finest handling of all the aircraft's Marks, the VIII had an excellent balance of power and maneuverability. American pilots in the Mediterranean heartily agreed with Quill's assessment and hated to give their Spitfires up for Mustangs in March 1944. *William Skinner*

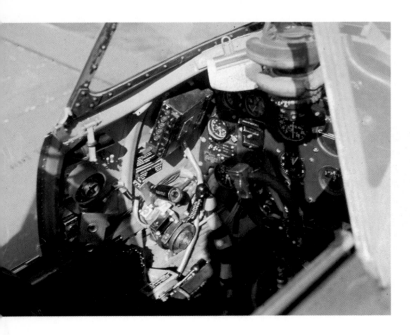

Almost all Spitfire cockpits were identical except for a few minor changes. This Mark VIII cockpit was usually filled by Bill Skinner, a 308th Squadron, 31st Fighter Group, pilot who flew P-40s in North Africa. Skinner transferred to the 31st and stayed with the group through most of its Spitfire tenure in the Mediterranean. *William Skinner*

A couple of "war-weary" Spitfires, a Mk VB (AR404) and a Mk VC (EN904), were handed over to the 7th Photo Group at Mount Farm, England, in late 1943, so its pilots could transition into the type before entering combat with their PR.XIs. The 7th was the Eighth Air Force's primary photo-recce outfit, flying Spitfires and F-5 Lightnings through the end of the war. *Robert Astrella*

A No. 16 Squadron Spitfire PR Mk XI rests on the grass at Melsbroek, Belgium, in the latter part of 1944, while the Allies were pressing through Europe toward Germany. The aircraft was fitted with an F24 short-focus camera under each wing for low-level reconnaissance. *RAF Museum*

These 7th Photo Group ground crewmen wait as the pilot of a PR.XI warms up his Merlin engine in the early morning light. Pilots of the 7th roamed across all corners of Europe, revealing what the Germans were up to and taking strike assessment photos of Eighth Air Force bombing missions. Staying at maximum altitude, around 40,000 feet, and maximum cruise was a recce pilot's best defense against enemy fighters, since he had no guns. *Robert Astrella*

The multiple-mission "camera" silhouettes painted on the side of this 7th Photo Group Spit PR.XI indicate it has seen its share of combat over Europe. Reconnaissance flying did not have the glamour of flying pure fighters, but it was a critical job, requiring enormous dedication and determination in the face of enemy opposition. *Robert Astrella*

Long after being a first-line fighter, a Spitfire LF.XVI (originally ordered as a IX) sits on the hardstand at Duxford in 1954. Those RAF pilots fortunate enough to still be flying Spitfires in the 1950s considered their jobs a secret worth keeping from their peers. Fortunately, the RAF considered saving such aircraft to fly for the public a trust, resulting in the formation of the Battle of Britain Memorial Flight. *Robb Satterfield*

Flying in battle dress, complete with a well-placed tie, was standard in the RAF during World War II. A pilot couldn't be better dressed to fly a new Griffon-powered Mk XIVC in 1944, and that five-bladed propeller caught the attention of everyone within eyesight. The jump in performance with the powerful Griffon engine was significant. *RAF Museum*

As an LF.IXE, ML417 went to the Indian Air Force in 1948 as a two-seat Tr.9 and was eventually stored in the service's Air Force Museum until sold to Sen. Norman Gaar in Kansas in 1971. Stephen Grey, originator of The Fighter Collection, bought it in 1980 and restored it to its original single-seat configuration. The aircraft has been a mainstay of the organization ever since. *T. Thomassin*

The oldest flying Spitfire in the world is Mark IA AR213, originally purchased by Air Commodore Allen H. Wheeler in October 1946. It passed through several owners, flew in the film *Battle of Britain* and ended up with its current owner, Blue Max Museum of Film Flying at Booker Aerodrome, England. *T. Thomassin*

Another Spitfire shipped to India, LF.VIIIC MT719, left the UK in 1947 and became an instructional airframe before being recovered by Ormond Haydon-Baillie in 1977. Italian Franco Actis bought the airframe in 1978 and got it back into the air as one of the very genuine warbirds to fly in Italy. In 1993, Jim Cavanaugh bought it for his Flight Museum in Addison, Texas, where it flies on a regular basis. *Jeff Ethell*

Another of Allen Wheeler's 1946 purchases, AB910, was an LF.VB that was raced, then purchased by Vickers-Armstrong in 1955 before being donated to the Battle of Britain Memorial Flight 10 years later. It flew in the film *Battle of Britain*, when it was damaged in a landing accident. Restored, it was damaged again in 1976, rebuilt, and put back in service with the BBMF, where it flies today. *Gerry Turner*

After service as an LF.IXE, TE308 was converted to a two-seat Tr.9 for the Irish Air Corps in 1951, then became an instructional airframe. Sold to take part in the *Battle of Britain* film, the aircraft later passed on to Don Plumb in Canada in 1970, who converted it to a single-seater by covering the rear cockpit. It went to the Owls Head Transportation Museum in Maine in 1975, was sold to Woodson K. Woods of Arizona in 1979, converted back to a two-seater, and finally sold to current owner William S. Greenwood of Aspen, Colorado, in 1983. *Christopher P. Davis*

Coauthor Jeff Ethell flies Rudy Frasca's FR.XVIII near the Frasca Air Museum, Urbana, Illinois. TP280 was another Spitfire passed to the Indian Air Force in 1947. The hulk was recovered by Ormond Haydon-Baillie in 1977, and Frasca bought it in 1978. After a very long restoration period, with work by both the Frasca Museum and Historic Flying at Audley End, the Spitfire was airborne again in 1992. Since that time it has been flown regularly, much of the time by late coauthor Ethell. *Choice Productions*

The prototype Griffon-engined Spitfire was DP845, initially rebuilt from a production Merlin-powered airframe and designated the F.IV. Later it became the F.XII, fitted with the Griffon IIB, then the IV, and finally the VI. Delays on availability of the Griffon doomed the Mk IV as a production variant, but when the engine's bugs were worked out, the Mk XII began to roll off the assembly line in late 1942. *NASM*

If the hydraulic system failed, the pilot would ensure that the landing-gear selector lever was in the DOWN position (this being essential) and push the emergency lowering lever forward and downward. The angular travel of the emergency lever was about 100 degrees for puncturing the seal of the cylinder and then releasing the piercing plunger; it had to be pushed through this movement and allowed to swing downward. No attempt would ever be made to return it to its original position until the spent cylinder was replaced.

For the wheel brakes, the control lever for the pneumatic brakes was fitted on the control column spade grip; differential control of the brakes was provided by a relay valve connected to the rudder bar. A catch for retaining the brake lever in the ON position for parking was fitted below the lever pivot. A triple pressure gauge, showing the air pressures in the pneumatic system cylinders and at each brake, was mounted on the left side of the instrument pane.

Machine Guns and Cannons

The eight Browning .303 machine guns on the Spitfire IIA were fired pneumatically by a

push button on the control column spade grip. The compressed air supply was taken from the same source as the brake supply, the available pressure being displayed by a gauge. The push button or trigger was surrounded by a milled sleeve, which could be rotated by a quarter-turn to a SAFE position, in which it prevented operation of the trigger. The SAFE and FIRE positions were engraved on the sleeve and could also be identified by touch, as the sleeve featured an indentation that was at the bottom when the sleeve was in the SAFE position and at the side when the sleeve was turned to the FIRE position.

The four .303 machine guns and two Hispano 20-mm cannons on the Spitfire Mk IIB were also fired pneumatically by a triple push-button or trigger mechanism of the control column spade grip. A milled finger lever extending from the bottom of the push-button casing provided the means for locking the trigger in the SAFE position, SAFE and FIRE being engraved on the adjacent casing. When the lever was in the FIRE position, a pip extended also from the top of the casing, enabling the pilot to feel the setting of the button.

To prevent accidentally firing the cannon on the ground, a safety valve mounted below the landing gear control unit in such a way that the cannon firing system was inoperative when the landing gear wheels were down and locked. For practice firing, however, a finger lever on the safety valve could be operated to allow the use of the firing system.

The cannons were cocked pneumatically by a cocking valve on the right side of the cockpit.

Gun Sight

For sighting the machine guns and cannons, a reflector gun sight was mounted on a bracket above the instrument panel. Below the mounting bracket were a main switch and a dimmer switch marked OFF, NIGHT, and DAY. Three spare lights for the sight were stowed in holders on the right side of the cockpit.

When the sight was used during the day, the dimmer switch would be in the DAY position to give full illumination, and if the background of the target was very bright, a sun-screen could be slid behind the windscreen by pulling on the ring at the top of the instrument panel. For night use, a low-wattage light bulb was brought into circuit, and the light could be varied by rotating the switch knob.

Gun Camera

A G.42B cine-camera was fitted in the leading edge of the left (port) wing, near the root end, and was operated by the cannon-firing button on the control column spade grip. A succession of exposures was made during the whole time the button was depressed, providing the camera selector switch on the left side of the cockpit was on.

A footage indicator and an aperture switch were mounted on the wedge plate above the throttle lever. The switch enabled either of the two camera apertures to be selected, the smaller aperture being used for sunny weather. A stowage clip was provided to receive the electrical cable when the indicator and switch were not fitted.

Radio Equipment

The Spitfire Mk IIA/IIB fighters were equipped with a combined transmitter-receiver, either type being TR 9D or TR 1133, and an R 3002 head set.

With the TR 9D installed, a Type C mechanical controller was fitted on the left side of the cockpit above the throttle lever, and a wireless remote contactor and contactor master switch were fitted on the right side of the cockpit. The master contactor was mounted behind the pilot's

headrest, and a switch that controlled the heating element was attached to the forward bracket of the mounting. The heating element had to be switched OFF when the pilot left the airplane. The microphone/telephone socket was located on the right side of the pilot's seat.

With the TR 1133 installed, the contactor gear and microphone/telephone socket were as for the TR 9D installation, but the Type C mechanical controller was replaced by a push-button electrical control unit.

Emergency Equipment

The cockpit canopy, or hood, could be jettisoned in an emergency by pulling the lever, mounted inside the top of the hood, in a forward and downward movement, and pushing the lower edge of the hood outboard with the elbows. On Spitfires not fitted with a jettisonable type of hood, a crowbar was provided to assist in jettisoning the canopy; the crowbar was mounted to a fixture on the inside of the entry door.

A forced landing flare was carried in a tube fixed inside the fuselage. The flare was released by means of a ring grip on the left of the pilot's seat.

Flying the Spitfire Mk IIA/IIB Fighters

The Rolls-Royce Merlin XII engine was to use 100-octane fuel, but with the reduced limitations, which are shown in brackets, it could burn 87-octane gas.

• • •

Powerplant Limitations (RPM & Boost)

	RPM	Boost lb/Sq in
Maximum takeoff to 1,000 feet	3,000	+ 12.5 (+ 7)
Maximum climbing 1 hr limit	2,850	+ 9 (+ 7)
Max rich continuous	2,650	+ 7 (+ 5)
Maximum lean continuous	2,650	+ 4 (+ 2-1/2)
Combat 5-minute limit	3,000	+ 12 (+ 7)

• • •

It should be clarified that + 12-pounds-per-square-inch combat boost had to be obtained by

A flight of FR.XIVs from the Royal Belgian Air Force Fighter School, Coxyde, form up for a postwar sortie. The Griffon-powered Spitfires were outstanding fighters, and many pilots considered the XIV the best Spitfire of them all for raw performance, while still retaining some of the original aircraft's handling. The equal of any wartime piston-engined fighter, the XIV was an excellent V-1 catcher, since it had a top speed well matched to the buzz bomb. *Decobeck via Alfred Price*

operating the boost control cut-out, and this was only effective up to an altitude of about 10,500 feet.

The maximum diving limitation was 3,600 rpm, and with the throttle open no less than one-third, 3,000 rpm could be exceeded for only 20 seconds. But during combat, if above 20,000 feet, 3,000 rpm could be used for periods not to exceed 30 minutes.

The maximum diving speed of the Mk IIA/IIB aircraft was 450 miles per hour. They were not to exceed 160 miles per hour with the landing gear down or 140 miles per hour with the flaps down.

Engine Controls

The throttle and mixture control levers were fitted in a quadrant on the left side of the cockpit. A gate was provided for the throttle lever in the takeoff position, and an interlocking device between the levers prevented the engine from being run on an unsuitable air/fuel mixture. Friction adjusters for these controls were provided on the side of the quadrant.

The automatic boost control could be cut out by pushing forward the small red-painted lever at the forward end of the quadrant.

As far as the propeller controls were concerned, the control lever for the de Havilland 20-degree pitch or the Rotol 35-degree pitch constant-speed airscrews were on the throttle quadrant. The de Havilland 20-degree propeller had a positive-course pitch position, which was obtained in the extreme aft position of the control lever, when the airscrew blades were held at their maximum-course pitch angles and the propeller functioned as a fixed airscrew.

In dealing with the radiator flap control, the flap at the outlet end of the radiator duct was operated by a lever and ratchet on the left side of

The American Packard-built Merlin engine was the only thing that set the Mk XVI apart from its British Mk IX brothers. By this point in the design of the aircraft, the bubble canopy, pointed rudder, and clipped wings were standard on many Marks. This particular machine, a Mk XVIE, was attached to the RAF Central Gunnery School after the war. *MoD via Alfred Price*

the cockpit. To open the flap, the lever had to be pushed forward, after releasing the ratchet by depressing the knob at the top of the lever. The normal minimum drag position of the flap lever for level flight was shown by a red triangle on the top of the map case attached next to the lever. A notch beyond the normal position in the aft direction provided a position of the lever when the warm air was diverted through ducts into the wings for heating the guns at high altitude.

The ignition switches were mounted on the left bottom corner of the instrument panel. The starter push button at the bottom of the instrument panel operated the L.4 Coffman starter and the booster coil. The control for reloading the breech was below the right side of the instrument panel, and was operated by slowly pulling on the finger ring and then releasing it.

Cockpit Arrangement and Gear

The pilot's seat was adjustable for height by means of a lever on the right side of the seat. A release catch was fitted to the right side, so the pilot could lean forward without unfastening his harness.

A portion of the hatchway on the left side was hinged so the pilot could enter the airplane

cockpit. The door catches were released by means of a handle at the forward end. Two-position catches were incorporated to allow the door to be partly opened before taking off or landing to prevent the canopy, or hood, from sliding shut in the event of a mishap.

The sliding canopy was provided with spring catches for holding it either open or closed; the catches could be released by two finger levers at the forward end. From outside, with the hood closed, the catches could be released by depressing a small knob at the top of the windscreen. Provision was made on the door to prevent the hood from sliding shut if the airplane overturned on landing.

A small knock-out panel was provided on the right side of the canopy for use in the event of the windscreen becoming obscured.

A floodlight was fitted on each side of the cockpit; they were dimmed by a switch immediately below the instrument panel.

Cockpit heating and ventilation was accomplished by a small adjustable flap on the right side of the instrument panel, opened by turning a knurled nut under the flap.

For oxygen, a standard regulator unit was fitted on the left side of the instrument panel, and a bayonet-type receptacle was on the right side of

The definitive wartime production Griffon Spitfire, the Mk XVIII, was a refined XIV. The FR.XVIII, like this one, carried not only armament but three cameras for low-level tactical reconnaissance work, giving the pilot and his commanders a number of options in combat. The aircraft had so much power, the pilot's manual warned the pilot to apply only half power on take-off, or the aircraft would cartwheel out of control. Once airborne, the pilot could apply full power. *Alfred Price*

the cockpit. A separate cock was provided in addition to the regulator.

A mirror providing a rearward view was attached at the top of the windscreen.

De-Icing Gear

For windscreen de-icing, a tank containing the de-icing solution was mounted on the left side of the cockpit directly above the bottom longeron. A cock was mounted above the tank, and a pump and a needle valve to control the flow of the liquid were mounted below the landing-gear emergency lowering control. Liquid was pumped from the tank to a spray at the base of the windscreen, from which it sprayed upward over the front panel of the screen.

The flow of de-icing liquid was governed by the needle valve, after turning the cock to ON and pushing the pump plunger down to its full extent. The plunger would return to the extended position on its own, and if required, it could be pushed down again. When de-icing was no longer required, the cock would be turned to the OFF position.

The Rolls-Royce Merlin Engine

Rolls-Royce Limited was created in the year 1906 by Charles Rolls and Henry Royce. At the beginning, it designed and built engines for its luxury automobiles, which it still does today. But in 1910, just four years after Rolls-Royce was founded, Charles Rolls started Great Britain's first military flying school, and in July of that year, while he was piloting a Wright Brothers' aeroplane, he was killed.

It was not until 1916 that Rolls-Royce produced its first aircraft engine—a 12-cylinder water-cooled 275-horsepower V-type called the Falcon. Rolls-Royce produced two more V-12s during World War I, the 360-horsepower Eagle and the 525-horsepower Condor.

Subsequently, through the year 1933, Rolls-Royce created several other V-12 engines for aircraft, which culminated with the 1,295-cubic-inch displacement Kestrel of 600 horsepower.

During 1933, using its Kestrel for a basis, Rolls-Royce initiated work on the much larger 1,649-cubic-inch V-12 engine (a difference of 354 cubic inches). In keeping with its flock of "bird"

Originally slated for production as an LF.IX, PK312 was turned into an early Griffon-powered Mk 22 with a small tail, serving as the prototype for other aircraft in the series, which began to roll off the assembly line in March 1945. *Alfred Price*

engines, the new engine was appropriately named Merlin. Per R-R's claim, the new Merlin was to develop as much as 1,000 horsepower, and to help it do so, it underwent a major redesign in 1935. The result was the 990-horsepower PV.12 of early 1936, just in time for the arrival of the Type 300 prototype.

From the time of the Spitfire prototype's premier flight on 5 March 1936 until the appearance of the last Merlin-type engine to be used by production Spitfires, all of which either turned single- or two-stage gear-driven superchargers to provide for high-altitude performance, the Merlin's horsepower ratings grew from the original 990 horsepower to more than 1,650 horsepower.

It is an established fact that an airframe can only be as good as its powerplant. It is also true that Spitfire had an excellent airframe. Thus, the Rolls-Royce Merlin engine became a classic. In fact, the Merlin is arguably the best liquid-cooled engine of World War II.

The British Merlin was similar to the American Allison V-1710, which used engine exhaust-driven turbosupercharging rather than gear-driven superchargers. But it was the Merlin V-1650, rather than the Allison V-1710, that would increase the overall performance of yet another outstanding fighter plane—the P-51 Mustang. And until the Merlin-powered "Stangs" appeared, the Spitfire reigned supreme among the allied forces' various fighter aircraft.

One version of the Rolls-Royce Merlin, the Mk 66, was manufactured under British authority in the U.S. by the Packard Motor Company as V-1650-3s and -7s for use in several versions of the P-51 and the Spitfire Mk XVI. To distinguish the Packard-made Merlins from the Rolls-Royce Merlins, the Packard-made Merlins were redesignated as the Mk 266s in England. And, the Packard V-1650-3 and -7 Merlins generated 1,380 and 1,490 takeoff horsepower, respectively.

But even though Rolls-Royce had a very good product with its Merlin, it did not rest on its laurels. For when the Spitfire Mk XIIs and Seafire Mk XVs began to fly, they were powered by the bigger, heavier, and more powerful Rolls-Royce Griffon series of engines.

The Rolls-Royce Griffon Engine

Using its very successful Merlin series of engines as the staring point, Rolls-Royce engineered a wider and deeper engine block for the installation of larger pistons and longer connecting rods to increase cubic-inch displacement, and thus horsepower. The magnified cylinder bore diameter and connecting-rod travel distance added up to an engine with a wicked displacement of 2,240 cubic inches. In its first production form, the Griffon II, it developed 1,735 takeoff horsepower. This was an instant growth of 590 cubic inches and an immediate uprating of 200 horsepower over the Merlin. So Rolls-Royce's new Griffon V-12 featured lots of horsepower and room for growth. The Griffon became the largest liquid-cooled V-12 engine to be produced in large number.

Beginning with the 1,735-horsepower Mk II and Mk IV engines in the Spitfire Mk XIIs, the Rolls-Royce Griffon engines were developing as much as 2,375 horsepower in the last of the Spitfire fighters, the Mk 22s and Mk 24s, and the final flocks of Seafire fighters, the Mk 46s and Mk 47s. What is more, the Griffon engine weighed about 600 pounds more than the Merlin engine; yet, even with its wider and deeper block, the Griffon was only about 6 inches longer than the Merlin. Although it was a larger and heavier engine, the Griffon kept the frontal area of the Spitfire and the Seafire within acceptable limits.

Another difference between the Merlin and the Griffon was that their crankshafts rotated in opposite directions, and so their propellers. The Merlin engines turned left or counter-clockwise, while the Griffon turned right or clockwise from a pilot's perspective. This difference, of course, altered the bearing of torque on the airframe. Where a Merlin-powered Spitfire would have a tendency to drop its starboard, or right, wing during takeoff, a Griffon-powered Spitfire would drop its port, or left, wing. To distinguish the two, Rolls-Royce issued odd serial numbers to the left-hand Merlins and even ones

The final version of the Spitfire, the Mk 21/22 (the two differed only in fuel capacity) served well into the 1950s. The basic shape had changed enough that these should have been renamed, but it was difficult to let that classic name go, something Supermarine finally did with the Spiteful. This Mk 22 flew with No. 607 (Auxiliary) Squadron . . . the No. 4 was an air-race marking, not a squadron number. *Alfred Price*

to the right-hand Griffons.

Both of these engines had a great deal of torque, which ultimately affects handling qualities. In an effort to all but eliminate this undesired twisting motion on Spitfire and Seafire airframes, both the Merlin and the Griffon engines were fitted with six-bladed, contra-rotating propeller systems. These were made up from two three-bladed propellers with 11-foot diameters. The idea was that if one propeller turned left and one turned right, torque would be canceled out, and the airframe would get a stable ride. The contra-rotating propeller system worked to a point, but not well enough to warrant total utilization on all versions of the Spitfire and Seafire aircraft.

In summary, during the Spitfire's and Seafire's development cycles, their Rolls-Royce Merlin and Griffon powerplants made them exceptional airframes, which resulted in their successes as great fighter planes.

The Wartime Production Effort

The Supermarine Division of Vickers-Armstrongs Limited must continue to be highly commended on its wartime production effort. For even after its Woolston factory had been reduced to rubble by enemy bombardment on 25 September 1940, its less than adequate Eastleigh

facility continued to produce the badly needed Spitfires. Having only built about 60 Spitfires from June to September 1940, additional production started to increase at Castle Bromwich. And by the end of 1940, including the few that had been built at Woolston (Southampton), 1,144 Spitfires had been built.

The so-called shadow factory at Castle Bromwich finished its first squadron-ready Spitfire on 22 August 1940. It had been preceded by some 40 nonready Spitfires, which, of course, were soon readied for combat and delivered to their squadrons. During the war, this factory near Birmingham became the biggest producer of Spitfires and Seafires, creating more than 12,000, or more than 50 percent of all that were built.

During its production life, Vickers-Supermarine and its complex assortment of subcontractors produced at least 26 distinct versions of the Spitfire and Seafire, in addition to numerous subvariants. Moreover, to keep them flying, Rolls-Royce produced 23 versions of its famed Merlin and at least 10 versions of its equally respected Griffon. And it was not until March 1949, almost 13 years to the day after the Type 300 had made its first flight, that the very last of these immortal fighters—a Seafire FR 47 (VR972)—rolled off its assembly line at South Marston.

Spittin' Fire:
Flying the Spitfire

Many of the classic World War II warbirds have survived to fly in this age—the Curtiss P-40 Warhawk, Republic P-47 Thunderbolt, Hawker Hurricane, Grumman F6F Hellcat, Chance Vought F4U Corsair, North American P-51 Mustang, Bell P-39 Airacobra, and P-63 King Cobra. Of them all, the Vickers-Supermarine Spitfire is definitely one of the most enjoyable to be aloft in, according to co-author Jeffrey L. Ethell (Fighter Writer).

The Spitfire series of fighter aircraft was unique. This is partly due to the many different versions being powered by two similar powerplants, the Rolls-Royce Merlin and Griffon engines. As these were liquid-cooled inline V-12 engines, the late models of the Spitfires sported 12 engine exhaust pipes protruding outward from their lengthy noses. These two powerful piston engines literally spewed out the hot fires they created within themselves. This was especially pronounced during nighttime operations.

Since it was Vickers-Supermarine chairman Sir Robert McLean who had insisted on the name Spitfire in early 1936, before the Type 300 prototype had flown and even though its designer, R. J. Mitchell, thought the name was "bloody silly," it was almost a sure bet that McLean's name would be approved by the British Air Ministry. And to Mitchell's dismay it was.

Nevertheless, as later proved in World War II combat, with as many as eight .303 machine guns or four 20-mm cannons and two .50-caliber machine guns belching and 12 exhaust pipes spewing out gas-fired flames, the airplane was indeed a Spitfire. The name proved to be a good one, now immortalized in aviation history.

Co-author Jeff Ethell flew both Merlin- and Griffon-powered Spitfires on a number of occasions. Several months before his untimely death in the crash of a Lockheed P-38 Lightning he was flying out of Tillamook, Oregon, on 6 June 1997 (the 53rd anniversary of D-Day), he shared his feelings on flying these fabulous birds of prey. Jeff was a renowned aviation history author and a stellar pilot. His report and others follow.

A Pilot Report
by Jeff Ethell

Walking up to a Spitfire is almost a religious experience for anyone who knows a shred about aviation history. For me, approaching this icon as a pilot about to fly it was definitely just such a feeling, not only for its good looks and legendary handling, but for its pivotal role in World War II. For this single aircraft was a symbol of Great Britain's refusal to give up during that dark summer and fall of 1940. In spite of the Hawker Hurricane's larger part in the Battle of Britain, the Spitfire won the hearts of both its pilots and its countrymen, taking on a far greater significance than that of a lifeless machine. Just to see those elliptical wings traverse the skies accompanied by the throaty roar of the Merlin engines did more for the British war effort than any song written to spur morale.

Most pilots get their first taste of a Spitfire through the Rolls-Royce Merlin-powered versions, the Mk IX in particular, and I was no exception. Compared to other World War II fighters, even Britain's own Hurricane, the Spitfire is very small. Packing that much horsepower into such a tiny airframe is indeed intimidating, leading to doubts of being able to control such a beast. On the other hand, next to their older Merlin-powered brothers the Rolls-Royce Griffon-powered Spitfires are long and lean, exuding a brute force, personified by a long snout with five-bladed propellers. Gone is the delicate nature of the older Mk Vs and Mk IXs.

Some bemoan this transformation as losing Reginald Mitchell's original purity of line, but I consider the Griffon-powered Spitfires beautiful machines in themselves. Their shape and 450-mile-per-hour speed puts them right up there with the most advanced piston-powered and propeller-driven fighters ever produced. Having flown both Merlin- and Griffon-powered versions, I find both unique and intoxicating aircraft.

Regardless of the version, all Spitfire cockpits are virtually identical and wonderfully compact. Climbing in a Spitfire cockpit really is (to use a very-worn phrase) like pulling the machine on. A quick scan of the instruments, knobs, and levers reveals them to be in just about the same places in all versions. The English-type blind flying panels are all identical, a feature which makes transition between the types very simple. Everything comes immediately to hand, particularly if one has flown Spitfires for awhile. This is a very comfortable and reassuring feeling. Once the pilot is strapped in, the cockpit door is put on latch (not fully closed) and the large Ground/Flight electrical buss switch on the right-hand side of the seat is thrown to FLIGHT (if a ground power unit is being used it would stay on GROUND). This arms the master switch on the instrument panel, which is flipped on, applying power to the airplane, and removes the bar guarding the magneto switches.

Pre-start checks: propeller rpm lever full forward, fuel cut-off (mixture) control full aft, check pneumatic pressure for 120 pounds minimum, undercarriage indicator light for down, flap selector up, main fuel cock on, check barometric static boost gauge reading (usually zero), fuel pressure warning light on, fuel low-level warning light out, undercarriage emergency lever in vertical position, radiator shutter control open. If everything is done correctly, the Spitfire is about the easiest World War II aircraft to start there is. Main fuel tank boost pump on for 30 seconds to prime the system then turn off, fuel cut-off full forward, two strokes on the primer for a normal day (None if the engine is warm . . . believe it! I got some exciting [exhaust] stack fires finding this out), ignition switches on, press starter and boost coil buttons simultaneously. The engine usually fires up within two blades and runs like a clock.

While the Merlin-powered versions run very smooth, the more powerful Griffon-powered variants feel as if they are angry. The sound from the exhaust stacks and the vibration transferred to the seat of the pants communicates visceral power, almost a desire to go kill something. Any high-performance car enthusiast would enjoy this sensation of unbridled horsepower, and as far as any high-performance fighter pilot is concerned, this creates an impatience to be turned loose for the hunt. Every fighter I've been in is great fun to fly, but only a few are brutally straight about why they exist. The Griffon-powered Spitfire is one such machine.

After a check for good oil pressure, move the throttle up to 1,200 revolutions per minute for warm up. Check to make sure pneumatic pressure is rising and that the fuel pressure and generator warning lights are out, then raise and lower the flaps to check the system. The pneumatic system (compressed air) operates the brakes, flaps, machine guns, radiator shutters, and supercharger change, so a thorough check of the entire system is mandatory (but in my case, *almost* the entire system, as the bird I'm in has no guns).

With enough warmth in the coolant and oil, a flip of the parking brake catch releases the brake lever on the spade control grip and the airplane is taxiing with minimal power. The first time I had the opportunity to fly a British airplane with this hand-operated air brake system, I was skeptical about it being very effective, compared to hydraulic toe brakes. Within a very few minutes though, I was completely won over. It was far easier to manage, particularly on engine run-up, when one has to really stand on most American fighter aircraft rudder pedals. If the rudder pedals are even, equal brake is applied on both sides; as one rudder pedal is applied then more brake pressure is fed to that side. Strength of application is delivered by the hand lever on the grip. The major benefit to all this is having one's feet and legs almost completely relaxed most of the time.

Short of the runway, parking brake catch back on, stick full back, and slowly . . . and I mean slowly . . . run up to barometric static, or zero, on the supercharger boost. Any rapid throttle movement or too much power will nose any Spitfire over in a heartbeat. Test supercharger, toggle each magneto for 100-rpm maximum drop, exercise the propeller, check generator light out. Power back for pretakeoff checks: elevator trim neutral, rudder trim full right (full left on the Griffon-powered machines . . . remember, their propellers turn the other way), check throttle friction, main tank fuel cock on, main boost pump on, flaps up, supercharger auto (red light out), carburetor air intake to clean air, harness locked, canopy open, taxi out onto the active runway.

Lining up for takeoff is intimidating with that long Rolls-Royce Merlin engine sticking way out in front . . . even more so with the Griffon. There is no sense in thinking too much about that though because that's just the way it is. Throttle up slowly to prevent a lurch to the left (if in a Griffon Spitfire, where the prop turns in the opposite direction [or clockwise from the pilot's view], the lurch is to the right). Right foot moves forward almost in concert with right hand to keep the nose straight down the runway and the right wing down. The Merlin-powered Spitfires are quite nice to handle on takeoffs, even with the power all the way up. The Griffon-powered Spitfires are something . . . monster torque shoves the right wing down rapidly, until full left aileron and full (give or take a minuscule amount) left rudder is held. The Griffon is more of a wounded lion with an eagle's wings bellowing horrendously, while the Merlin is more like taking a magic carpet ride.

In either version there is enough raw power and noise to keep any pilot tightly focused on keeping everything under control. Actual liftoff at around 80 or 90 knots goes by almost unnoticed. Switch hands, move the landing-gear lever down to disengage it from the slot, inward through the gate, and then smartly all the way forward, hold momentarily, then let go. If all is well, the lever snaps outward through the upper gate, then springs back into the upper slot. It's easy to spot a new Spitfire pilot . . . the plane porpoises as the pilot changes hands and works the gear lever. As all this is happening, power is brought back to climb settings while speed is held at something like 150 knots. Place the radiator shutters in automatic, secure the entry door, pull the canopy shut (crank it shut in the full bubble-canopy Griffon Spits), dial out a little of the rudder trim, and get used to seeing the vertical speed indicator point toward the top.

Sitting behind that massive V-12 engine pumping out so much power is intoxicating. The earth falls away at a rapid rate, at least for something with a propeller. A look around reveals the excellent visibility out of both the abbreviated and the full bubble canopies. This lessens, to a degree, the impression of being engulfed by a Spitfire,

though the feeling of actually being part of the machine does not change. Level off, reduce to cruise power, and retrim. All the trimmers are powerful and sensitive, so it doesn't take much to overcorrect. The machine is neutrally stable laterally and stable elsewhere, unless too much yaw is cranked in, whereupon longitudinal trim changes drastically. The elevator is very light, while the rudder is stiff and the ailerons are even stiffer.

Every Spitfire I've flown takes a bit more muscle to roll than most other types of fighter aircraft. As speed increases, both rudder and ailerons get heavier, resulting in a curious mismatch at high speed—one has to handle the almost oversensitive elevators with a light fingertip touch while arm wrestling the stiff ailerons. Pilots had to keep this in mind during combat, particularly when going up against the F-W 190, which had a sterling rate of roll and exceptionally well-harmonized flight controls. That being said, the Spitfire is very well-balanced and delightful to maneuver. Aileron rolls at 190 to 200 knots are crisp and easily controlled, while loops at 280 to 300 knots, with all that pull out front, are great, soaring, vertical challenges to the sky. And nothing, except maybe a Zero, can outrun a Spitfire. With those light elevators, one can pull the fighter effortlessly around as tight as one wishes in a circle, with the only limits being lack of power to sustain the turn or blackout due to excessive G forces.

Much to my continual appreciation, the aircraft stalls like a Piper Cub. Though a wing tends to drop, there isn't the slightest mean streak in it unless you cob the power, which produces a violent torque roll. Power off, gear and flaps down, main fuel tanks full, most versions of the Spitfire stall at around 65 knots. In the landing pattern, reduce speed to 140 knots, harness locked, check brakes off and pneumatic pressures, fuel main tank cock on, supercharger red light out, boost pump on, canopy open.

Switch hands, move the landing-gear lever forward out of the slot and hold for about two seconds, pull it inward through the upper gate and then full back in one smooth movement. The lever should spring outward through the lower gate . . . once the wheels are locked down, the lever will automatically spring into the lower slot. During the cycle, the quadrant window will show UP or DOWN, but once the lever is seated in either slot, the window should show IDLE. To check gear down, there is a small green window on the panel that will light up DOWN, and you should see the small mechanical rods, which stick up through the wing tops. Toggle the flap butterfly switch on the upper left of the instrument panel to DOWN . . . the split surfaces go all the way down very fast . . . then set engine rpm to 2,600.

With that enormous snout out in front of me, I try to make a 100-knot curving approach to landing in order to keep the runway in sight as long as possible. (One has to wonder just how difficult it was for the Royal Navy chaps to land on the decks of aircraft carriers in their Seafires.) By the time I'm rolling out across the field boundary, if at maximum landing weight, I should be no faster than 85 knots with power and 95 knots in a glide. At lighter weights, these speeds can be reduced five knots.

All Spitfires are exceptionally easy to land, with no inherent tendency to swerve or groundloop. Just reduce power to idle, flare to a three-point attitude, and she sets down on a feather almost every time. This is a great surprise, considering the narrow-track undercarriage and a full-swivel, nonlocking tailwheel. Why doesn't it drop a wing violently or make the pilot stomp on the rudder pedals, you might ask. I wish I knew. The genius of managing to combine light-aircraft handling characteristics with such a high-performance machine is nothing short of miraculous, compared to most other World War II tail-dragger types.

One or two landings in the Spitfire and you are in love for life. It makes you look like a hero to your peers every time . . . unless you ignore the manual speeds and come in too fast. Then it's a beast! Instead of settling down gently on three points, it floats, skips, and generally gets very upset. As a result, wheel (main gear) landings are not a very wise option. One of the finest demonstrations of these characteristics is the telefilm *Piece of Cake*, which has some excellent close-ups of Spitfires taking off and landing.

Off the runway and stop . . . check sufficient pneumatic pressure for taxiing, flaps up, boost pump off, radiator shutters open. Once at dispersal, fuel cut-off full aft, magneto switches off, all electrics off, master switch off, brakes off, entry door open . . . get your helmet off and breathe in some of that burnt oil bouquet . . . better than the finest wine. For a Spitfire is something to be savored, no matter what vintage.

Spitfire LF Mk VIIIC
by Flight Lieutenant Donald K. Healey (Don), No. 17 Squadron, 1944–46

I arrived on No. 17 Squadron in Burma, having come from the Middle East, where I had flown Hurricane Mk IIs, Spitfire Mk Vs, and Spitfire Mk VIIIs. By the time I turned up in-theater in 1944, No. 17 Squadron had been flying Spitfires for a few months. The old squadron pilots who had become attached to the venerable Hurricane since the early days of the Burma campaign were very impressed with the sleek Spitfire. One facet of the aircraft that they particularly appreciated was the Spitfire LF Mk VIIIC's armament of two Hispano 20-mm cannons and two Browning .50-caliber machine guns.

The selection mechanism for choosing one or the other weapon in combat couldn't have been easier, as on the spade grip in the cockpit, the fire selector button was vertically arranged on a rocker system. If you pressed the top part you got machine guns, if you pressed the bottom part you got cannons, and if you pressed the middle part you got the lot. This made the aircraft ideal for both ground strafing and aerial combat.

On one particularly memorable sortie, I was in a two-aircraft section with Flight Lieutenant Ted Marshal (DFC), an Australian who commanded "B" Flight—and he spotted a recently reroofed "basha" (hut) on the edge of the jungle while on patrol. Marshal was a very experienced tactical reconnaissance pilot and could spot things moving under the jungle canopy better than anyone on the No. 17 Squadron—he even adapted his flying "outlook" to facilitate target spotting. This meant he kept his eyes on the ground at all times, leaving me to handle the skies above the horizon.

On the mission in question, we each took it in turns to strafe the hut, trying to set it on fire, and on my second pass the grass roof slid back and I came face to face with a multi-barreled pom-pom anti-aircraft gun! Just as they took aim to fire, my starboard cannon seized and the recoil from the still-firing port 20-mm cannon threw my Spitfire into a side-slip to the right and I skidded sideways barely 10 feet over the top of the hut. This involuntary maneuver obviously put the Jap gunners off their aim, as they missed me by some margin—I could see their astonished faces as I sped over the top of the "basha," and no doubt they could see my equaling wide-eyed gaze through the canopy.

I climbed back up to 2,000 feet and reported my sighting to Ted, who suggested returning to Meiktila to inform our dive-bombing friends in No. 28 Squadron of our discovery. They duly scrambled a dozen Hurricane Mk IICs and we guided them back to the target, which they destroyed.

With our mix of [two] cannons and [two] heavy-caliber machine guns, we were always in demand to help clear the stubborn Japanese ground forces from the path of the steadily encroaching 14th Army. Our Spitfires carried enough ammunition for a minute-and-a-half length burst, which may not seem like a lot. However, it is amazing the effect a well-aimed short squirt had on the Japs. We would always fit a few tracer rounds in the magazines about 50 shells from the end of the ammunition supply to tell us how much we had left in each type of weapon. Japanese fighter pilots soon cottoned on to this during aerial duels, and due to their invariably superior numbers, would jump on the first Spitfire to fire tracers. Our response was to get the squadron armorers to feed tracers into our ammo belts several rounds into our supply, which certainly caught a number of "Oscar" pilots out!

Don Healey was in the RAF from February 1941 until December 1946, when he returned home from Japan. Just before VJ-Day, his squadron was the first to deploy outside of Hiroshima just after it had been atomic bombed. He is currently the honorable secretary for the pilots and officers of No. 17 Squadron (Spitfires).

Busting the Doodlebugs
by Flight Lieutenant Charles S. Allen (Charlie) (RAF)

One of my jobs while serving with the RAF in World War II was to bust the Doodlebugs. It wasn't what I thought I'd be doing but turned out to be a unique experience, because up until the time, I never heard of a pilotless airplane.

Germany's dreaded flocks of V-1 buzz bombs were every bit as chicken shit as their cowardly dictator was. And as Hitler was himself a self-centered murderer, the V-1s were also cold-blooded killers of many hundreds of innocent civilians. It was for this reason that some of us in the RAF got the job of trying to stop these terrible weapons before they reached their intended targets, which were in most cases populated. Oddly enough, my first sortie against these pilotless pulse-jet powered flying bombs came on 24 July 1944—my 21st birthday! Some birthday present.

At the time I was serving with RAF Group No. 11, Squadron No. 610 at West Malling. I was assigned to a relatively new Griffon-powered Spitfire Mk XIVE, which was able to burn a special 150-octane petrol, which allowed me to operate the motor with up to 25 pounds per square inch of boost on the supercharger for increased speed

over some of the Mk XIVs in service. My Spitfire could fly in excess of 450 miles per hour where the other Mk XIVs struggled to hit 435 miles per hour. My squadron had been at this since June 1944, with a great deal of success. But this was a brand-new type of warfare, and we were forced to learn how best to deal with it as we went along.

The Doodlebugs, as we nicknamed those dreaded V-1s, generally operated at altitudes ranging from 200 to 4,000 feet at speeds of 350 to 450 miles per hour. Therefore, since our Spitfires could easily match their altitudes, and didn't have an impossible problem in chasing them down, we joked about how they were so small and how they seemed to doodle along; thus, their nickname.

My Spitfire was equipped with the "E," or Universal Armament, wing, which had two British-made 20-mm Hispano cannons and two .50-caliber American-made Browning machine guns (one of each in either wing). And with its maximum speed of 450-plus miles per hour at 26,000 feet it easily outclassed the Mk XIVC from which I had recently transitioned.

Generally speaking, my new Mk XIVE was fast enough to intercept these robot bombs, and was heavily armed enough to kill them. But shooting at them, as it turned out, wasn't such a good idea. For if you did, as was so rudely discovered by some of our chaps, their warheads could explode and mortally wound both you and your plane.

So we developed and used two other tactics: 1. We would fly in close, place one of our wingtips under one of its wingtips, then sharply bank away from it. This maneuver would send it out of control to a crash, but would likely cause at least some damage to our planes. 2. We would move in close, and place one of our wingtips above one of its wingtips. This maneuver would destroy the V-1's lift and send it out of control to a crash, but in this case, it wouldn't cause any damage to our planes. It was the latter tactic we preferred and used more often than not.

In any event, on my very first Operation Noball mission, I didn't even see a V-1. But on subsequent sorties I saw far too many of those bloody bastards. Personally, I busted nine of them by the time Germany wasn't able to launch them anymore. Mostly by flipping them, whereby, luckily enough for yours truly, my aircraft never sustained any serious damage.

I learned later that the RAF had destroyed more than 1,900 V-1s in just four months (between June and September 1944), and that Germany had actually launched some 8,600 of the little shits. In the end, the V-1s alone accounted for at least 2,400 deaths and some 7,100 serious injuries to my fellow countrymen in and around London. It's no telling just how many other V-1s might have been launched if their launch sites hadn't been destroyed by the time they were. A lot of the V-1 launch sites were destroyed by Spitfire Mk XIVCs, each packing one 500-pound bomb and two 250-pound bombs, in fighter-bomber sorties.

In conclusion, I just what to say that I'm very happy to be one of the chaps that was able to bust at least some of those thoughtless Buzz Bomb bastards. And in doing so, though I remain uncertain, I would be pleased to know that I might have saved at least some lives.

Some Words and Useful Information
by Group Captain David J. Green (RAF, Retired), Founder and Chairman of the Spitfire Society

According to Group Captain David J. Green, "After, say, 1943, the air-defense role (i.e., pure fighter work) declined, due partly to the lack of offensive operations by the Luftwaffe, and partly to the more mobile nature of the conflict. Indeed, most of my operations during my second tour in the Mediterranean were concerned with very steep (60 degrees) dive-bombing and ground-attack work with the Spitfire. But my first tour, starting around El Alamein in Egypt, was spent in the night-fighter business flying [Hawker] Hurricane Mk IICs."

In sharing two pages from his log book, which covers 10 days of his combat activities during 20 to 30 March 1945, "which are typical of many recorded during World War II," David Green then of No. 281 Wing, No. 73 Squadron of the Balkan Air Force, provided this information:

1. On 20 March he performed a 45-minute air test.
2. On 22 March he flew four flights: a one-hour flight to Prkos; a 45-minute flight to bomb Gospic; a one-hour flight to bomb Gospic again and nearby roads; and a one-hour and 30-minute road reconnaissance flight to Senj.
3. On 23 March he performed a 20-minute air test.
4. On 24 March he flew two flights: a one-hour and five-minute flight to Prkos; a one-hour and 30-minute flight intended to escort a Douglas DC-3, but bad weather forced a return to base.
5. On 25 March he flew three flights: a 50-minute flight to Prkos; a two-hour and 25-minute flight to escort a Douglas DC-3 to Lavada; and a one-hour and 30-minute flight to bomb Otoka.
6. On 26 March he flew a 35-minute flight on an intended bombing mission but had to return to base because of bad weather.
7. On 28 March he flew a one-hour and 25-minute flight to bomb Otoka.
8. On 29 March he flew two flights: a 50-minute flight to bomb Ostrazak; a one-hour and 15-minute flight to Ostrazak again and Otoka.
9. On 30 March he flew four flights: a one-hour and 15-minute flight to bomb Gospic; a one-hour and 20-minute flight to bomb Krupa; a 50-minute flight to bomb Ostrazak; and a 55-minute flight to bomb Ostrazak again, but bad weather forced a return to base.

During most of the above missions, Green encountered lots of light and heavy flak from anti-aircraft artillery pieces, including a direct hit on 22 March. On 26 March, due to bad weather, he had to jettison his bombs into the Adriatic Sea prior to his return to base. And on his second of four flights on 30 March, during his bombardment of Krupa, he happily exclaimed: "Wonders will never cease—no flak!"

Group Captain David Green was born in Axminster, England, in 1922. Early in 1945 (to better explain his personal situation during and after the above time period), he joined No. 73 Squadron in Yugoslavia as a flight commander, and after VE-Day, he returned to England. He retired from the RAF in 1977 at the age of 55. He is a director of the R. J. Mitchell Memorial Museum Limited, and he founded the Spitfire Society in 1984. A marvelous entity in the world of aviation.

One of the many accomplishments of the Spitfire Society was the creation of an exact replica of the original Type 300 prototype (K5054), so the world's many, many Spitfire lovers can behold the true beauty of Mitchell's best example of what a small, light, and powerful fighter should be like in early 1936. So now, thanks to the extraordinary effort of the Spitfire Society and its faithful members, the very first Spitfire—which had crashed to destruction much earlier, has been recreated as it first appeared for all to enjoy.

My First Mission in a Spitfire
by Pilot Officer Tony N. Ross (RAF)

It was 15 October 1944, after only some 20 hours on Spitfires—a Mk XIVC for the most part—when I finally reached my goal. For this was when I got to fly my first mission as a fighter pilot with No. 401 Squadron's B Flight. Ten days earlier, on 5 October, it was this squadron that became the first allied unit to shoot down a jet-powered Messerschmitt Me 262 fighter. Apparently, I knew exactly what squadron to get assigned to!

I was strapped into my Griffon 65-powered Spitfire F Mk XIVC with its five prop blades turning, as B Flight taxied out for launch. We were to fly sweep over the [English] Channel, and after rendezvous, assist with the escort of an unspecified number of Yank B-17s that would be returning from their bombardment runs high above the V-2 rocket facility at Pentamünde.

We were extended outward from one another in battle formation to protect the big "Forts" [B-17 Flying Fortresses], which were now ahead of us but still out of sight. The sky was blue but the clouds below us were thick and gray. Then we saw the "Forts" in large numbers below us, above those very clouds, and my radio became filled with chatter.

One voice was directed at me: "Spiderweb-three (my call sign), there's a plane coming up on your 6 o'clock (on my tail)."

I broke right. A single-engine fighter came in under me before I knew what had happened, and he was firing his guns. By rights, he should have hit me. It was a Focke-Wulf 190, which immediately dived into the clouds below us and got away. There I was, armed to the teeth with four guns and two cannons, and I never even got off one single burst.

After we had returned to base, my commanding officer called me aside and barked, "Ross, you should be dead. Starting right now, and from now on, you've got to check your own ass." I was more than embarrassed because, from day one, that is exactly what they tell you to do: "LOOK ALL AROUND, ALL THE TIME!"

I really was quite fortunate on that first mission more than 54 years ago, but believe me, I did indeed watch my own ass from then on.

So I did much better in the ensuing days of the war, but I never really became anything more than a mediocre fighter pilot (two confirmed Me 109 kills and one Me 210 probable). And after the war, I returned to the job that I knew best, that of supporting my family, and wound up being a bank manager in Liverpool. And before you ask the question I've been asked a hundred times before: No, I never met even one of the Beatles. They must have banked elsewhere.

Photo-Recce Work in a Spitfire PR Mk XI
by Squadron Leader William A. Benn (Billy) (RAF, Retired)

Before I get into this, please be kind enough to let me say something I've wanted to say for more than 50 years, but never really had the nerve to say: I was literally scared to death every damn time I went up on a mission! I personally believe my fellow unarmed photo-recce lads were just as scared, but brave as they acted (and still do, I guess), they just didn't admit to the fear they had in that bloody war. At least never to me. But let me tell you, there's nothing quite like flying an unarmed and often unescorted airplane into a full-fledged combat zone where you can't defend yourself. Now that I finally have that off my conscience, I'll now proceed with one story I recall.

I was assigned to No. 16 Squadron, 2nd Tactical Air Force, in the north of France in late 1942. At the time, I occupied a very new Spitfire PR Mk XI (its log book showed 4.5 flying hours). When it was equipped with a belly tank, it became a long-range airplane capable of flying some 2,000 miles, and with its 400-plus-miles-per-hour speed, it was an extremely fast airplane as well. The reason it was so fast, I remember being told at the time, was its new type of Rolls-Royce Merlin engine—a 1,520-horsepower Merlin Mk 61. But the airplane had one major problem as far I was concerned: It didn't have any armament! Oh, how I wished I could have been assigned to an armed photo-recce Spitfire, but that was never to be. We were constantly told that if we did our mission properly, and used our escorts when they were provided to us, that we would have a relatively good go at it. Boy, were they wrong.

On one mission in particular on 3 December 1942, as I recall, our job was to photograph the German shipping port of Bremerhaven for bomb damage assessment. Flying out of our French base at Amiens, we headed eastward over Belgium. It would be a long flight and our flight plan called for us to fly at an altitude of 12,000 feet, at best cruise speed, which in this case was about 280 to 300 miles per hour. It was a good thing we had belly tanks, because this round trip would cover a great many miles.

Luckily, we were scheduled to rendezvous with some American P-51s for our protection. But as fate would have it, they never showed up. To this very day, I don't know why they never did; they must have had pressing business elsewhere. In any event, we flew on to Bremerhaven and took our bloody pictures, without any trouble whatsoever. But on our way back, our good luck suddenly changed.

As we approached the Belgium town of Tilburg, we were met by two Messerschmitt Me 109s. And suddenly our four unarmed PR Mk XIs became those proverbial sitting ducks. What was really strange to me at the time, as I recall, is that they, too, were flying at a pretty low altitude. I guess they were at 13,000 feet or so. But not for long, because they saw us, and here they came.

As soon as we saw them, we jettisoned our belly tanks and made left-hand climbing turns to reach a better maneuvering altitude—about 17,500 feet, as I remember. At that altitude we could be a bit more agile, and more importantly, we could increase our speed. We figured that maybe we could outrun them. No, we figured we *had to* outrun them. For with our 400-plus-miles-per-hour speed, we thought, we might be able to leave them behind.

As we desperately climbed, so did they. And being right on our tails, they, of course, were firing at us. And right off, I got hit with a pretty good volley of whatever it was I was getting hit with. Smoke was billowing from my engine compartment, I couldn't see where I was going, and down I went to try to find a clear area for a landing. As I felt my way down, hoping the smoke would go away so I could see again, it got worse. Now oil was on my windscreen, and I decided I had better get out before I crashed into the ground. After a struggle with my restraints, my entry door, and canopy, and after I had rolled inverted, I bailed (rolled back and off the wing). I made a hard but good landing on both feet, but I broke my left ankle, as it turned out. Even though I was in a lot of pain, I quickly realized just how lucky I was in the minutes that followed, for I soon was rescued by some French soldiers instead of being captured by the Jerries.

After my return to England and my recovery, I rejoined my squadron and saw the war out. But in conclusion, it was that very mission that shows you exactly why I hated to fly unarmed aircraft in combat situations.

Sadly, two of the chaps in my flight that day were killed. The other made it safely back to base. So as you can see, two armed fighters did in three out of four unarmed photo-recce planes. And personally, I believe we could have faired much better if we could have flown that mission with armament.

Carrier Decks to Sandy Beaches
by Peter Alexander (RN)

After starting my life in the Royal Navy, I was first placed into service in a Seafire Mk XV in July 1944. It was powered by a giant 1,850-horsepower Rolls-Royce Griffon engine, and I personally had it out to 426-miles-per-hour indicated air speed at 18,235 feet over the Bay of Bengal between India and Burma. I was aboard the HMS *Stalker*, assigned to No. 809 Squadron. And at the time, we mostly flew strafing sorties against Jap installations on the numerous sandy beaches we encountered during our sailings throughout the bay.

Then in late April 1945, we started to fly combat air patrols to bolster the allied landings in and around Rangoon, Burma, during Operation Dracula. Officially this operation lasted from 30 April to 2 May 1945, and during those three days, as part of the 21st Carrier Group, we never participated in any aerial combat. Instead, once again, all we did was make strafing run after strafing run on Japanese-held fortifications. We usually hit them with a pair of 250-pound bombs and most all of our ammunition before returning to our carrier.

Since I had been fully prepared to do battle with the Jap fighters I'd heard so much about, I was at a loss to know just where in the hell they were, especially the newer ones like the Raiden. But after nearly a year of being on station, and prepared to fight, I hadn't even seen a Jap aircraft of any sort.

Then suddenly we got the word that the war was over. We had heard that we'd be fighting for a much, much longer time. Well into 1946 and even 1947, it was rumored. We had been led to believe that the only way we were going to defeat the Japs was to invade their islands. Not a good thought. But all of a sudden, thank God, that terrible ordeal was finally over. I know this doesn't make for exciting reading, but this Seafire fighter pilot didn't even get one chance to shoot at one Jap fighter. And I often wonder if maybe that isn't a good thing. Because, a lot of our guys did get to shoot at them, and a lot of them aren't here to talk about it.

158-plus Hours in a Seafire Mk IIC
by Henry Morgan

I logged a bit over 158 hours in a Seafire Mk IIC, serving aboard the HMS *Furious* with No. 801

Squadron from August 1944 to July 1945. We operated throughout the Mediterranean, but stayed pretty close to the Sea of Crete during most of our tenure. Our primary mission was to seek and destroy any enemy shipping around Greece.

The Seafire Mk IIC was quite maneuverable with good forward vision, but at 110- to 120-miles-per-hour approach speed—as required at certain times—you were very near to being below safe speed; we usually landed at 140 to 150 miles per hour. If you lost your engine during approach (very unlikely), the airplane could not be controlled because of the drag of the dead engine's propeller and the variable winds across the deck. At 135 miles per hour, you could compensate. A friend who joined No. 801 Squadron when I did had this happen to him upon returning to the carrier after a mission. My friend lost his engine while approaching the deck. He didn't make it, crashed into the sea and was rescued.

The large-diameter four-bladed propellers on the Rolls-Royce Merlin 32-powered Mk IICs cleared the deck by only about a foot. In a carrier landing, compression of the undercarriage struts (oleos) would bring the propeller blade tips within inches of hitting. In one case I sat on an accident review board where this had happened. We determined the port landing gear had been a bit too low when filled during servicing, and a hard landing—within normal range—caused the propeller to dig into the carrier's deck.

With supercharger boost the Mk IIC flew very well indeed. It was easy to fly, and it was maneuverable. The roll and climb rates were exceptional, and it was a very agile plane. It was much more responsive than the Seafire Mk IB, and I enjoyed flying it.

Flying the Spitfire
by Michael Spencer (RAF)

In May 1945, the Vickers-Supermarine Spitfire was a somewhat aged aircraft but there were still many of them in service in the air forces throughout the world, including those Seafires in the naval forces. But we loved our Spitfires nevertheless.

Near Southampton was a U.S. Army Air Forces base, equipped with American P-38 Lightnings. Those chaps were equally impressed with their fighters. Somehow, somewhere, the inevitable discussion occurred, and it turned into a challenge match between a P-38 and my Spitfire Mk F XVIII. After I flew in the contest was set, and on that day in May, a large crowd of American and British personnel had gathered for the spectacle.

Both of our fighters, side-by-side at the end of the runway, fired-up. After we signaled that we were ready, we were given the GO. My Spitfire could pull 60 inches Hg manifold pressure and could skid tires with brakes locked at full power. I cleared the runway in a very short run of about 100 feet, sucked up my landing gear, climbed slightly to about 150 feet, then made a tight 180-degree turn at the far end of the field and made an opposite-course (head-on) pass at the Lightning, which had just reached the cross runway area. At that point the P-38 was off the runway and had just retracted its landing gear. Incidentally, the cross runway area of the field was no more than 60 percent of the length of the runway used. Embarrassed, the P-38 pilot turned around the field once and immediately landed.

I landed but wasn't finished. Starting from a standstill, engine screaming, at the GO, I took off and climbed to about 10,000 feet in under two minutes. That's over 5,000 feet per minute! My airplane, powered by a two-stage Griffon 67 of 2,340 takeoff horsepower, had acceleration and climb like no other Spitfire I had flown.

In May 1953, just after my recall during the Korean War, I arrived on base where I checked-out in a Spitfire F.24 as part of my new duty. I hadn't flown anything in two years. The pilot's handbook listed maximum landing-gear retraction and extension air speed as 135 miles per hour, as I remember. This was my first flight:

I cranked up that 2,375-horsepower Griffon 85 with contra-props at the end of the runway, checked the mags [magnetos], let go the brakes, and added more throttle to about 52 inches Hg manifold pressure. Before I could get my wits about me, I was off the ground in a slight climb, and when I looked over at the air-speed indicator, I found I was already at 135 miles per hour and still accelerating rapidly. I snapped up the landing-gear handle and reduced power. This was one hot airplane! Guaranteed to make you open your eyes wide and make your pulse race.

A friend of mine once told me that he checked-out in a Spitfire F.24 along with another re-tread pilot. The other pilot was so shaken by his first takeoff experience that he immediately landed and gave up flying. I can't say anything about that since this was a second-hand comment to me. The preceding two stories, however, are true from an eye-witness and first-person experience. Mine.

The Spitfire F.24, though it wasn't used in World War II, was, in my eyes, the epitome of World War II combat maneuvering design. Its overpowering Griffon engine, installed in a relatively small airframe, made it the ultimate point-defense fighter. It was quick, it was rugged, it was nearly viceless, except for certain tendencies associated with an extremely high-powered, highly

[wing] loaded performance aircraft. At the top of its speed range, in a dive (more than 450 miles per hour indicated), it wanted to tuck its nose under. This was always accompanied by buffeting, a warning that longitudinal control might be lost if speed were increased. On approach, under 150 miles per hour, it would drop a wing immediately—even with its contra-props, after violent stick shudder. With the gear down, this same phenomenon occurred at 110 miles per hour. Nevertheless, if flown within the guidelines, the aircraft would almost land itself.

On takeoff with the Spitfire F Mk XVIII on the other hand, without contra-props, problems such as torque roll could swiftly become manifest if care was not taken with the throttle that fed fuel to the engine. This aircraft, as well as the F.24-streaked skyward like a rocket, and this combination of heart-stopping speed and agility was not for novices. Nevertheless, despite their sterling performances, both of these Spits were for the most obsolete by 1946. Enter the jet age.

In one-on-one encounters with the Gloster Meteor, Spitfires, of course, were bested in every case. With both types of aircraft being flown by experienced pilots, no version of the Spitfire could ever take the initiative. The Meteor literally flew circles around them and could begin or break off combat whenever it chose. But remember, we didn't have any Meteors in the summer of 1940.

As the ultimate World War II dogfighting machine in RAF inventory then, the Spitfire was the best of its class. But in the end, it fell prey to Great Britain's efficiency, for the engineering minds that created it had done their work so well with its successors, that by the time the Spitfire was at the top of its growth potential, there were no more enemies to conquer.

FOREIGN USERS

Throughout the whole of World War II, which for the British peoples lasted from September 1939 to September 1945, many different versions of the Spitfire were taken into combat action by a myriad of dedicated pilots from a number foreign

countries. This joining of friendly forces was the direct result of Hitler's invasion schemes and tactics, whereby he left little choice in the matter. As more and more nations were overtaken by the so-called Third Reich, or were being threatened for such a takeover, their current air forces—which did not have much in the way of combat aircraft to fight with—voluntarily joined forces with England. And what was to become a long drawn-out, six-year air war was on.

These reluctant, yet chivalrous volunteers joined forces with the RAF, which, from late 1940 on, made sure there were enough Spitfires to go around. By the end of the war, no fewer than 13 friendly air forces had flown tens of hundreds of combat missions against the Axis powers. These included the United States, Belgium, Brazil, China, Czechoslovakia, Denmark, France, Greece, the Netherlands, Norway, Poland, Russia, and Yugoslavia.

These volunteer pilots fought on a daily basis in every area of confrontation—the European; Mediterranean; China-Burma-India; Dutch East Indies; North, Central, and South Pacific; and the North, Central, and South Atlantic theaters of operations.

The cockpit of a Mark I, the first production Spitfire, looked very much like the last of the line 10 years later. With only a few differences, all Spitfire and Seafire cockpits were wonderfully similar, giving pilots an immediate leg up in moving through the various Marks. The major item that appeared only in early Mark I cockpits was the hand pump on the right to raise and lower the landing gear. *Vickers via Alfred Price*

By the 1950s, the Spitfire had become an advanced trainer, like this Indian Air Force FR.XVIII. It was hard to believe pilots with so little flying time could be turned loose in a fire-breathing Griffon Spitfire, but as long as throttle movement was cautious, the aircraft handled beautifully, with a docile nature common to all Marks. *USAF*

Some of these pilots had joined up when there was little else to do; that is, to get a job and make money to support their families when work was scarce. Other pilots, like the American volunteers of the RAF's Eagle Squadrons, came aboard early in the fray to help Great Britain when the United States was idling in neutral, much as it did before its entry into the previous war.

These initial RAF Eagle Squadrons—the 71st, 121st, and 133rd, had become hardened combat veterans by the time the United States had shifted into gear and finally entered the war. These squadrons, flying Spitfire Mk VB fighters at the time, and the American volunteer pilots operating them, were transferred to the U.S. Army Air Forces, which in turn spawned the 4th Fighter Group, which became the genesis of Europe's mightiest air armada—the Eighth Air Force. The 4th Fighter Group's newly established fighter squadrons—the 334th, 335th, and 336th—retained their Spitfires until they were ordered to transition to the American-made Republic P-47 Thunderbolt beginning in March 1943. While the 4th Fighter Group grew to appreciate their new "Jug" fighter planes, its pilots had at first hated to part with their Spitfires.

The "Fourth but First" fighter group was not only the first American fighter group to use the Spitfire, it became the only U.S. Spitfire-equipped fighter group to remain on English soil. This was due to its greater amount of combat experience with the Spitfires. And while two other American fighter groups (the 31st and 52nd) also operated Spitfire Mk VBs in England, they were reassigned to the 12th Air Force in the Mediterranean Theater of Operations or MTO to participate in Operation Torch, the allied invasion of North Africa.

During 1941 and 1942, many other pilots from the British Commonwealth nations—especially Australia, Canada, and New Zealand—were assigned to RAF fighter groups/squadrons to operate the Spitfire. And as the RAF acquired adequate numbers of new Spitfires for the defense of England itself, the Royal Australian Air Force (RAAF), the Royal Canadian Air Force (RCAF), and the Royal New Zealand Air Force (RNZAF), were able to get their own flocks of Spitfires.

The Royal Canadian Air Force, for example, established numerous Spitfire-equipped units. In part, these RCAF units included the No. 127 Squadron (2nd Tactical Air Force), No. 401

A Royal Belgian Air Force Mk IX serves out its final military days, long after the RAF had finished flying Spitfires. Foreign air forces were often the source of derelict Spitfires for collectors and pilots who wanted to find examples for restoration. The 1968 gathering of Spitfires for the film *Battle of Britain* was a turning point for the survival of the breed. This Mk IX is currently one of the 50 or so airworthy Spitfires in the world. *Alfred Price*

"Ram" Squadron, No. 402 "Winnipeg Bears" Squadron, No. 403 "Hornet" Squadron, No. 411 "Grizzly Bears" Squadron, No. 417 "City of Windsor" Squadron, and No. 442 "Caribou" Squadron, which primarily fought in the European Theater of Operations.

It was a long time before Spitfire production equaled the number of pilots who wanted to fly and fight in them. But by mid-1943, thousands of Spitfires were being operated by allied pilots.

When World War II ended, Vickers-Supermarine had pumped out nearly 22,800 Spitfires and Seafires. Many of each type survived the war and were procured by postwar users to bolster their air forces.

Many of these friendly air forces did not relinquish them until they too could afford turbojet-powered fighters These nations, including India, Greece, Portugal, Spain, Thailand, Norway, Denmark, the Netherlands, Italy, Pakistan, and Sweden, thought highly of their World War II veteran fighters.

Thus today, these nations and others proudly display some of their Spitfires and Hooked Spitfires in their museums. Wonderfully, throughout the world, as many as 50 Spitfires are still flying.

These Norwegian PR.XIs, being fueled in the 1950s, are at the very end of their service lives, slated to be replaced by jets. Pilots flying them enjoyed being the last of a breed, but soon the aircraft would be sold or scrapped. Only decades later did buyers begin to look for them as sport aircraft. *USAF*

With landing gear and flaps extended this Mark XIX is on final approach. *Alfred Price*

This Mark IX with No. 129 Squadron was turned over to the Italian Air Force on 26 June 1947, where it was flown for several years. Like most Spitfires, it disappeared into the cold-hearted maw of military progress. To find such an aircraft today would be akin to uncovering King Solomon's mines, for it is now a fact that a Spitfire, of any type, is literally worth more than its weight in gold. *Alfred Price*

RETIREES AND SURVIVORS

Great Britain was the second nation to successfully investigate the feasibility of developing and producing aircraft that were exclusively powered by gas turbine or turbojet engines. This began with the Gloster E.28/39 Pioneer, a single-seat, single-engine fighter-type airplane, which made its first flight on 15 May 1941. This significant development quickly led to England's ongoing research into the full production of such aircraft. And by the end of World War II, on a limited scale, it was already producing the Gloster Meteor, a twin-engine fighter, and the de Havilland Vampire, a single-engine fighter, both powered by turbojet engines. Their first flights were in March and September 1943, respectively.

Subsequent successes in jet-powered aircraft soon spelled doom for England's piston-powered and propeller-driven fighters, and forced the retirement of two of its best, the Spitfire and Seafire.

The early transitions from piston- to turbojet-powered fighter planes in Great Britain started slow but was in full swing by the late 1940s and early 1950s. Even though the Spitfire and Seafire were extensively used in postwar assignments, it had become obvious that both had been overtaken by progress.

The last operational mission for an RAF Spitfire, specifically a Spitfire PR Mk XIX of No. 81 Squadron, was logged on 1 April 1954 in Southeast Asia. Subsequent to this mission, Spitfires at last entered their retirement.

In reference to the Royal Navy Seafires, after the Seafire Mk 47s of No. 800 Squadron had completed their duties in the Korean War, they were retired from first-line service. Then in 1957,

after they had been employed by training squadrons of the Royal Navy Reserves, the Seafires were retired.

Production ended in March 1949, almost 13 years to the day from the premier flight of the Type 300 prototype, when the final version, a Seafire FR 47 (VR972) exited the factory at South Marston. During that incredible production run, Vickers-Supermarine produced 27 major versions and a number of subvariants of the Spitfire and Seafire aircraft. These aircraft were powered by at least 20 versions of the Rolls-Royce Merlin, with takeoff horsepower ratings running from about 1,000 to 1,600 horsepower. Some were powered by a minimum of 10 versions of the Rolls-Royce Griffon, with takeoff horsepower ratings ranging from about 1,700 to 2,300 horsepower. A total of 20,751 Spitfires and 2,408 Seafires were manufactured in Great Britain, for a grand total of 23,159 aircraft.

Whether these great planes were used for low-, medium-, or high-altitude combat missions, for armed and unarmed photographic reconnaissance and mapping duties, or to simply deliver beer to thirsty ground-pounders, they were (and are) highly respected. (Spitfires are known to have carried two kegs of beer, one under either wing, on their bomb racks!)

These train and plane killers, tank and ship destroyers, troop and truck busters were all-around fighters, fighter-bombers, and fighter-interceptors that earned the right to be in the top-five warbirds of World War II. Fortunately, a large number of aircraft museums have preserved numerous survivors.

Museum Pieces

Many Spitfire survivors reside throughout the United Kingdom and the commonwealth, as well as in dependencies, or reside other nations. A number of these surviving Spitfires are listed here by their location, Mark and serial numbers, and military markings:

Type 300 Prototype

Although it is not a survivor per se, the Spitfire prototype lives on in the original markings of its manufacturer. To celebrate the 60th anniversary of its first flight, the Type 300 prototype (K5054) was re-created and shown in March 1996 by the Spitfire Society. It currently resides at the society's facility in Southampton.

Spitfire Mk I

Royal Air Force Museum, Hendon, England; Spitfire Mk IA (K9942); No. 72 Squadron (SD-F)

Museum of Science & Industry, Chicago, Illinois, United States; Spitfire Mk IA (P9306)

Science Museum, London, England; Spitfire Mk I (P9444); No. 72 Squadron

Imperial War Museum, London, England; Spitfire Mk IA (R6915); No. 609 Squadron

Royal Air Force Museum, Hendon, England; Spitfire Mk IA (X4590); No. 609 Squadron (PR-F)

Spitfire Mk II

Australian War Museum, Canberra, Australia; Spitfire Mk IIA (P7973); R-H

Canada War Museum, Ottawa, Canada; Spitfire Mk IIB (P8332); ZD-L

Royal Air Force Battle of Britain Memorial Flight, Coningsby, England; Spitfire Mk II (P7350); No. 266 Squadron

Dumfries and Galloway Aviation Museum, Scotland; Spitfire Mk II (P7540); No. 312 Squadron

Spitfire Mk V

Museum of Science and Industry, Manchester, England; Spitfire Mk VB (BL614); No. 611 Squadron (ZD-F)

Yugoslavian Aviation Museum, Belgrade, Yugoslavia; Spitfire Mk VC (JK448)

Royal Air Force Wattisham, Suffolk, England; Spitfire Mk V (EP120); No. 501 Squadron

Shuttleworth Collection, Old Warden, England; Spitfire Mk V (AR501); No. 310 Squadron

Manchester Air and Space Museum, Manchester, England; Spitfire Mk V (BL614); No. 611 Squadron

Royal Air Force Linton-upon-Ouse, Yorkshire, England; Spitfire Mk V (BM597); No. 315 Squadron

Royal Air Force Battle of Britain Memorial Flight, Coningsby, England; Spitfire Mk V (AB910); No. 222 Squadron

Spitfire Mk VII

National Air and Space Museum, Smithsonian Institution, Washington, District of Columbia, United States; Spitfire Mk VIIC (EN474)

Spitfire Mk VIII

South African National Museum of Military History, Johannesburg, South Africa; Spitfire Mk VIII (JF294); No. 5501

Royal Air Force St. Athan, South Wales; Spitfire Mk VIII (MT818); No. 315 Squadron

Spitfire Mk IX

Museum of Science and Industry, Birmingham, England; Spitfire Mk IXC (ML247); ST-A

Warbirds of Great Britain Limited, Blackbushe, near Yately, Hants, England; Spitfire Mk IX (NH238); No. 84 Group Support Squadron

Royal Air Force St. Athan, South Wales; Spitfire Mk IX (MK356); No. 443 Squadron

Duxford Airfield, Cambridge, England; Spitfire Mk IX (MH434); No. 222 Squadron

Militaire Luchtvaart Museum, Soesterberg Air Base, The Netherlands; Spitfire Mk IXC (NJ143)

Aviodome Museum, Amsterdam-Schiphol, Holland; Spitfire Mk IXC (NJ271); H-53

Hellenic Air Force Museum, Tatoi Air Base, Greece; Spitfire Mk IXC (MJ755)

Champlin Fighter Museum, Mesa, Arizona, United States; Spitfire Mk IX

Musee Roal de L'Armee, Brussels, Belgium; Spitfire Mk IXC (MJ783); GE-B

Museu Storico Dell' Aeronautica Militaire Italiana, Vigna de Valle Air Base, Italy; Spitfire Mk IX (MK805); A-32

Mingaladon Air Base, Rangoon, Burma; Spitfire Mk IXE (ML119)

Museo do Ar, Alverca Air Base, Lisbon, Portugal; Spitfire Mk IXC (ML255); MR-2

Danmarks Flyvemuseum, Billund, Denmark; Spitfire Mk IXC (NH417)

Military Museum Kbely Airport, Prague, Czech Republic; Spitfire Mk IXE (TE565); No. 310 Squadron (NN-N)

Spitfire Mk XI
United States Air Force Museum, Wright-Patterson Air Force Base, Dayton, Ohio, United States; Spitfire PR Mk XI (PA908); 7th Photo Group, United States Army Air Forces

Flysamlingn, Gardermoen Air Base, Norway; Spitfire PR Mk XI (PL979)

Castle Donington, England; Spitfire PR Mk XI (PL983); No. 1 Pilot's Pool Squadron

Spitfire Mk XIV
Whitehall Theater of War, London, England; Spitfire Mk XIV (MV370); No. 39 Motor Unit

Luftfahrtmuseum, Hanover, Germany; Spitfire Mk XIVC (MV370); EB-Q

Classic Air Displays, Elstree, England; Spitfire Mk XIV (NH904); No. 414 Squadron

Museum of Science and Industry, Manchester, England; Spitfire Mk XIVE (MT847); No. 6 Motor Unit (AX-H); see immediately below

Royal Air Force Aerospace Museum, Cosford, England; Spitfire Mk XIVE (MT847); No. 6 Motor Unit (AX-H); final location of above

Warbirds of Great Britain Limited, Blackbushe, near Yateley, Hants, England; Spitfire Mk XIV (SM832); No. 222 Motor Unit

Warbirds of Great Britain Limited, Blackbushe, near Yateley, Hants, England; Spitfire Mk XIV (MV293); No. 33 Motor Unit

Rolls-Royce Limited, Castle Donington, England; Spitfire Mk XIV (RM689); Air Fighting Development Unit

Spitfire Mk XVI
City Museum, Stoke-on-Trent, England; Spitfire Mk XVIE (RW388); OU-U

Royal Air Force Manston, Kent, England; Spitfire Mk XVI (TE752); No. 66 Squadron

San Diego Aerospace Museum, San Diego, California, United States; Spitfire Mk XVIE (SL574); ND-T

Royal Air Force Museum Storage, Royal Air Force Cardington, England; Spitfire Mk XVIE (SL674); No. 501 Squadron

Western Canada Aviation Museum, Winnipeg, Canada; Spitfire Mk XVIE (TE214)

Royal New Zealand Air Force Museum, Wigram Air Base, New Zealand; Spitfire Mk XVIE (TE288); OU-V

Royal Air Force Leuchars, Fife, England; Spitfire Mk XVI (TB252); No. 329 Squadron

Royal Air Force Museum Storage, Royal Air Force Cardington, England; Spitfire Mk XVIE (SL764); No. 501 Squadron

Royal Air Force Central Flying School, Leeming, England; Spitfire Mk XVI (TE356); No. 501 Squadron

Royal Air Force Exhibition Flight, Abingdon, England; Spitfire Mk XVI (TB382); No. 602 Squadron

Royal Air Force Exhibition Flight, Abingdon, England; Spitfire Mk XVI (TE311); LZ-V

Royal Air Force Coltishall, Norfolk, England; Spitfire Mk XVI (SL542); No. 595 Squadron

Royal Air Force Credenhill, Hereford, England; Spitfire Mk XVI (TE392); No. 126 Squadron

Warbirds of Great Britain Limited, Blackbushe, near Yateley, Hants, England; Spitfire Mk XVI (RW386); No. 604 Squadron

Ulster Folk and Transport Museum, Hollywood, County Down, England; Spitfire Mk XVI (TE184); No. 6 Motor Unit

Royal Scottish Museum of Flight, East Fortune, North Berwick, Scotland; Spitfire Mk XVI (TE462); No. 33 Motor Unit

Royal Air Force Northolt, Middlesex, England; Spitfire Mk XVI (TE476)

Royal Air Force Uxbridge, England; Spitfire Mk XVI (RW382); No. 6 Motor Unit

Royal Air Force Sealand, Clwyd, England; Spitfire Mk XVI (TD248); No. 695 Squadron

Royal Air Force Cosford, England; Spitfire Mk XVIE (RW393); No. 203 Advanced Flying School

Spitfire Mk XVIII
Indian Air Force Museum, Palam Air Base, New Delhi, India; Spitfire Mk XVIIIE (SM986); No. 6 Motor Unit

Spitfire Mk XIX
Royal Air Force Brawdy, Dyfed, England; Spitfire Mk XIX (PS915); No. 541 Squadron

Royal Air Force Museum Storage, Royal Air Force Cardington, England; Spitfire PR Mk XIX

Royal Air Force Battle of Britain Memorial Flight, Coningsby, England; Spitfire PR Mk XIX (PM631); No. 6 Motor Unit

Royal Air Force Battle of Britain Memorial Flight; Spitfire PR Mk XIX (PS853); Central Photographic Reconnaissance Unit

Flygvapenmuseum, Linkoping, Sweden; Spitfire PR Mk XIX (PM627)

Royal Thailand Air Force Museum, Bangkok, Thailand; Spitfire PR Mk XIX (PM630)

Spitfire Mk 21

Royal Air Force Wittering, England; Spitfire Mk 21 (LA255); No. 1 Squadron (JX-U)

Royal Air Force Museum Storage, Royal Air Force Cardington, England; Spitfire Mk 21 (LA198); No. 1 Squadron

Spitfire Mk 22
Royal Air Force Binbrook, Lincolnshire, England; Spitfire Mk 22 (PK664); No. 615 Squadron

Royal Air Force Abingdon, Oxfordshire, England; Spitfire Mk 22 (PK624); No. 33 Motor Unit

Spitfire Mk 24
R. J. Mitchell Hall, Spitfire Museum, Southampton, England; Spitfire Mk 24 (PK683); No. 47 Motor Unit

Royal Air Force Museum, Hendon, England; Spitfire Mk 24 (PK724); No. 33 Motor Unit

Seafire Survivors
In addition to the Spitfire survivors listed above, there are several known Seafire Mk XVs on static display. These are as follows:

Mingaladon Air Base, Rangoon, Burma; Seafire Mk XV (PR376)

Meiktila Air Base, Burma; Seafire Mk XV (PR422)

Canadian Air Force Base, Calgary, Alberta, Canada; Seafire Mk XV (PR451); VG-AA-N

Airworthy Spitfires
Added to the many surviving Spitfires and Seafires on display throughout the world, there are, as of this writing, something on the order of 50 flying examples around the world, which are, for the most part, privately owned. That so many Spitfires still take to the skies so long after World War II is, in large measure, due to the wonderful 1968 gathering of them for the epic film *Battle of Britain*. Even though a dozen or so of these legendary fighters were airworthy, many more were used for set dress-

ing, or were restored to simply run their engines at low power, in order to taxi in front of the cameras. When the filming of the movie had been completed, most of the aircraft were offered up for sale at ridiculously low prices, and most of them found good homes. And now as the 20th century ends, restoring and flying Spitfires has taken on the trappings of a major industry.

Following is a list of all *known* airworthy Spitfires as of this writing, by owner, location, Mark and serial number, and military markings:

Spitfire Mk I
Proteus Petroleum Limited, Wycombe Air Park, England; Spitfire Mk IA (AR213); No. 609 Squadron (PR-D)

Spitfire Mk II
Royal Air Force Battle of Britain Memorial Flight, Royal Air Force Coningsby, England; Spitfire IIA (P7350); No. 72 Squadron (RN-S)

Spitfire Mk V
Royal Air Force Battle of Britain Memorial Flight, Royal Air Force Coningsby, England; Spitfire Mk VB (AB910)

Historic Aviation Collection, Audley End, England; Spitfire Mk VB (BM597); No. 317 Squadron (JH-B)

The Fighter Collection, Duxford Airfield, Duxford, England; Spitfire Mk VB (EP120); No. 402 Squadron (AE-A)

The Shuttleworth Collection, Old Warden Aerodrome, England; Spitfire Mk VC (AR501); No. 310 Squadron (NN-A)

Alpine Fighter Collection, Wanaka Airfield, New Zealand; Spitfire Mk VC (AR614); No. 312 Squadron

Spitfire Mk VIII
Cavanaugh Flight Museum, Dallas, Texas, United States; Spitfire Mk VIIIC (MT719); No. 17 Squadron (YB-J)

Mr. Jack Erickson, Tillamook Air Museum, Oregon, United States; Spitfire Tr.8 (MT818)

Mr. Robs Lamplough, Filton Airfield, Bristol, England; Spitfire Mk VIIIC (MV154); No. 145 Squadron (ZXZ-M)

Mr. Colin Pay, Scone, New South Wales, Australia; Spitfire Mk VIIIC (NV239); A58-758

Indian Air Force Historic Flight, Palam Airport, New Delhi, India; Spitfire Mk VIIIC (NH631)

Spitfire Mk IX
Mr. David Price, Museum of Flying, Santa Monica, California, United States; Spitfire Mk IXC/E (MA793); JE-J

Old Flying Machine Company, Duxford Airfield, Duxford, England; Spitfire Mk IXC (MH434)

Misters Maurice and Peter Bayliss, Bruntingthorpe Airfield, Leics, England; Spitfire Tr.9 (MJ627); No. 441 Squadron (BG-P)

Mr. David Pennell, Staverton Airport, Glos, England; Spitfire Mk IXE (NJ730), No. 32 Squadron (GZ-?)

Dutch Spitfire Flight, Deelen Air Base, The Netherlands; Spitfire Mk IX (MK732); No. 485 Squadron (OU-U)

Mr. Cliff Robertson, Kalamazoo Aviation Museum, Kalamazoo, Michigan, United States; Spitfire Mk IXC (MK923); No. 126 Squadron (5J-Z)

Mrs. Carolyn Grace, Duxford Airfield, Duxford, England; Spitfire Tr.9 (ML407); OU-V

The Fighter Collection, Duxford Airfield, Duxford, England; Spitfire Mk IXE (ML417); No. 443 Squadron (21-T)

Warbirds of Great Britain Estate, Fort Lauderdale, Florida, United States; Spitfire Mk IXE (NH238)

Mr. Kermit Weeks, Fantasy of Flight Museum, Polk City, Florida, United States; Spitfire Mk IXE (PL344)

Mr. Bill Goldstein, Lakeland, Florida, United States; Spitfire Tr.9 (PT462); No. 233 Squadron (SW-A)

Mr. Rick Roberts, Goodwood Airfield, West Sussex, England; Spitfire Tr.9 (PV202); No. 412 Squadron (VZ-N)

South African Air Force Museum, Waterkloof Air Base, Pretoria, South Africa; Spitfire Mk IXE (TE213); No. 1 Squadron, South African Air Force (AX-K)

Mr. Bill Greenwood, Aspen, Colorado, United States; Spitfire Tr.9 (TE308); RJ-M

Israeli Air Force Museum, Be'er Sheva Air Base, Israel; Spitfire Mk IXE (TE554); Israeli Defensive Air Force (57)

Historic Aircraft Collection, Duxford Airfield, Duxford, England; Spitfire Mk IXE (TE566); No. 312 Squadron (DU-A)

Spitfire Mk XI
Mr. Christopher Horsley, Duxford Airfield, Duxford, England; Spitfire PR Mk XI (PL965); No. 16 Squadron

Warbirds of Great Britain Estate, Fort Lauderdale, Florida, United States; Spitfire PR Mk XI (PL983)

Spitfire Mk XIV
The Fighter Collection, Duxford Airfield, Duxford, England; Spitfire Mk XIVE (MV293)

Mr. David Price, Museum of Flying, Santa Monica, California, United States; Spitfire Mk XIVE (NH749)

Mr. Bob Pond, Planes of Fame East, Minneapolis, Minnesota, United States; Spitfire Mk XIVC (NH904); No. 80 Squadron (W2-P)

The Fighter Collection, Duxford Airfield, Duxford, England; Spitfire Mk XIV (SM832); No. 17 Squadron (YB-A)

Spitfire Mk XVI
Mr. Bernie Jackson, Hollister Airport, Hollister, California, United States; Spitfire Mk XVIE (RW382); No. 604 Squadron (NG-C)

Mr. Woodson K. Woods, Carefree Airport, Arizona, United States; Spitfire Mk XVIE (SL721); WK-W

Alpine Fighter Collection, Wanaka Airfield, New Zealand; Spitfire Mk XVIE (TB863); No. 453 Squadron

Mr. Eddie Coventry, Earls Colne, England; Spitfire Mk XVIE (TD248)

Myrick Aviation, Jersey, Channel Islands, United Kingdom; Spitfire Mk XVIE (TE184)

Evergreen Ventures, McMinville, California, United States; Spitfire Mk XVIE (TE356); DE-D

Hockey/Treloar Syndicate, Towoomba, Australia; Spitfire Mk XVIE (TE384)

Mr. Kermit Weeks, Fantasy of Flight Museum, Polk City, Florida, United States; Spitfire Mk XVIE (TE476)

Spitfire Mk XVIII
Warbirds of Great Britain Estate, Fort Lauderdale, Florida, United States; Spitfire Mk XVIIIE (SM969)

Frasca Air Museum, Urbana, Illinois, United States; Spitfire Mk XVIIIE (TP280); No. 60 Squadron (Z)

Spitfire Mk XIX
Royal Air Force Battle of Britain Memorial Flight, Royal Air Force Coningsby, England; Spitfire PR Mk XIX (PN631); No. 618 Squadron

Euan English Estate, North Weald Airfield, England; Spitfire PR Mk XIX (PS853)

Royal Air Force Battle of Britain Memorial Flight, Royal Air Force Coningsby, England; Spitfire PR Mk XIX (PS915)

(The Spitfire Tr.8 and Tr.9 aircraft listed above were modified two-seaters that were used in postwar Royal Air Force training squadrons.)

Conclusion

Throughout its lengthy dealings with Germany and its warring cohorts, the United Kingdom heavily relied upon one of the best all-around fighter aircraft in the world to help defeat Hitler's Germany, Mussolini's Italy, and Hirohito's Japan. This was the Vickers-Supermarine Spitfire, and its Seafire offspring, and as history records, the right plane at the right time. Fighting in concert with the likes of the Hawker Hurricane, P-38 Lightning, P-47 Thunderbolt, and P-51 Mustang, the RAF Spitfire continually showed its prowess in aerial combat.

Not to forget its navalized spin-off, the Vickers-Supermarine Seafire series of carrier-based fighters, which likewise ran through the gauntlet of the war to emerge as yet another classic warbird. These immortal fighters were operated by the air forces of England, Australia, Belgium, Canada, Czechoslovakia, France, the Netherlands, Norway, New Zealand, Poland, Russia, South Africa, and the United States.

There is no doubt that the mild-mannered aeronautical genius, Reginald J. Mitchell, would have been extremely proud of his creation's important contribution to his country's survival.

R. J. Mitchell's passing came close to that of one of America's best-known advocates of air power, General William Mitchell (Billy), who died just 16 days before the Type 300 prototype's first flight. Coincidentally, with the Atlantic Ocean between them, these two men named Mitchell had a common goal—to win future conflicts with superior aircraft and exceptional air forces to man them. Both of these greats got their wish.

APPENDICES

APPENDIX A: SPITFIRE PRODUCTION AT A GLANCE

Mark Number	Number Built	Powerplant(s) and Primary Mission
Mk I	1,566	Merlin II; fighter
Mk II	920	Merlin XII; fighter
Mk III	1	Merlin XX; experimental
Mk IV	2	Griffon IIB; experimental
PR Mk IV	229	Merlin 46, 50/50A, 55, or 56; photographic reconnaissance
Mk V	6,464	Merlin 45, 46, or 50/50A; fighter
Mk VI	100	Merlin 47 or 49; fighter
Mk VII	140	Merlin 61 or 64; fighter
Mk VIII	1,658	Merlin 61, 63/63A, 66, or 70; fighter
Mk IX	5,665	Merlin 61, 63/63A, 66, or 70; fighter
Mk X	17	Merlin 64 or 77; fighter
PR Mk XI	471	Merlin 61, 63, or 70; photographic reconnaissance
Mk XII	100	Griffon II or IV; fighter
PR XIII	18	Merlin 32; photographic reconnaissance
Mk XIV	957	Griffon 65 or 66; fighter
Mk XVI	1,054	Merlin 266; fighter
Mk XVIII	100	Griffon 65 or 67; fighter
FR Mk XVIII	200	Griffon 65 or 67; photographic reconnaissance
FR Mk XIX	225	Griffon 65 or 66; photographic reconnaissance
Mk XX	1	Griffon 65; experimental
Mk 21	122	Griffon 61 or 64; fighter
Mk 22	278	Griffon 85; fighter
Mk 24	54	Griffon 61 or 85; fighter
Total:	*20,351*	

Appendix B: Seafire Production at a Glance

Mark Number	Number Built	Powerplant(s) and Primary Mission
Mk IB	166	Merlin 50; fighter
Mk IIC	372	Merlin 32; fighter
Mk III	1,220	Merlin 55M; fighter
Mk XV	390	Griffon VI; fighter
Mk XVII	200	Griffon 61 or 65; fighter
FR Mk XVII	32	Griffon 61 or 65; photographic reconnaissance
Mk 45	50	Griffon 61; fighter
Mk 46	12	Griffon 61; fighter
FR Mk 46	12	Griffon 61; photographic reconnaissance
Mk 47	100	Griffon 87 or 88; fighter
FR Mk 47	40	Griffon 88; photographic reconnaissance
Total:	*2,408*	

Appendix C: Battle of Britain Groups, Squadrons, and Bases of Operation as of 8 August 1940

Group Number	Base of Operation	Squadron Number
No. 12	Duxford	No. 19
No. 13	Hornchurch	No. 41
No. 11	Hornchurch	No. 54
No. 11	Kenley	No. 64
No. 11	Hornchurch	No. 65
No. 12	Coltishall	No. 66
No. 13	Acklington	No. 72
No. 11	Hornchurch	No. 74
No. 11	Pembrey	No. 92
No. 13	Warmwell	No. 152
No. 12	Kirton-in-Lindsey	No. 222*
No. 11	St. Eval	No. 234**
No. 12	Wittering	No. 266
No. 13	Drem	No. 602
No. 13	Dyce	No. 603***
No. 11	Middle Wallop	No. 609
No. 11	Biggin Hill	No. 610
No. 12	Digby	No. 611
No. 13	Leconfield	No. 616

* No. 222 Squadron was converting to Spitfires at the time.
** One section of No. 234 Squadron was at Hullavington at the time.
*** The B Flight detachment of No. 603 Squadron was at Montrose at the time.

APPENDIX D: UNITED STATES ARMY AIR FORCES SPITFIRE GROUPS AND SQUADRONS, 1942–44

Group	Squadron	Time Period	Area of Operations
4th Fighter	334th	42–43	ETO
	335th	42–43	ETO
	336th	42–43	ETO
7th Photo	13th	43–45	ETO
	14th	43–45	ETO
	22nd	43–45	ETO
	27th	43–45	ETO
31st Fighter	307th	42–44	ETO/MTO
	308th	42–44	ETO/MTO
	309th	42–44	ETO/MTO
52nd Fighter	2nd	42–44	ETO/MTO
	4th	42–44	ETO/MTO
	5th	42–44	ETO/MTO
67th Recon	12th	43–44	ETO
	107th	43–44	ETO
	109th	43–44	ETO
	153rd	43–44	ETO

APPENDIX E: UNITED STATES ARMY AIR FORCES SPITFIRE COMBAT TOTALS, 1942–44

Sorties	Combat Losses	Enemy A/C Destroyed	Loss Rate Per Sortie
28,981*	191	256	0.7

* USAAF Spitfires dropped 212 tons of bombs.

Appendix F: Royal Air Force Merlin-Powered Spitfire Marks, Squadrons, and Area of Operations

Mark Number	Squadron Number	Area of Operations
Mk I and/or II	91, 92	England
	118	
	122, 123	
	129, 130, 131, 132	
	137	
	145	
	258	
	303	
	308	
	310	
	312, 313	
	315	
	331, 332	
	340	
	349, 350	
	401	
	403	
	411, 412	
	416, 417	
	452	
	457	
	485	
Mk IV	140	England
	541, 542	
	544	
	680, 681	
	683	
Mk V	19	England
	26	
	41	
	63, 64, 65, 66	
	71	
	74	
	91, 92	
	118	
	121, 122, 123, 124	
	127	
	129	
	131, 132, 133	
	136	
	164, 165, 166	
	222	
	234	
	302, 303	
	306	
	308	
	310	
	312, 313	
	315, 316, 317	
	322	

Mark Number	Squadron Number	Area of Operations
	331, 332	
	340, 341	
	345	
	349, 350	
	401, 402, 403	
	411, 412	
	416	
	421	
	441, 442, 443	
	451, 452, 453	
	457	
	485	
	501	
	504	
	521	
	595	
	602, 603	
	607	
	609, 610, 611	
	615, 616	
Mk V	32, 33	Middle East
	43	
	72	
	80, 81	
	87	
	93, 94	
	111	
	126	
	145	
	152	
	154	
	185	
	208	
	225	
	229	
	232	
	249	
	253	
	318	
	417	
	601	
Mk V	54 (Australia)	Far East
	136	
	607	
	615	
Mk VI	118	Far East
	124	
	521	
	602	
	616	
Mk VII	32	Far East
	41	
	92	
	124	

Mark Number	Squadron Number	Area of Operations	Mark Number	Squadron Number	Area of Operations
	131			452, 453	
	133			457	
	152			485	
	417			501	
	485			504	
	602			521	
	616			595	
Mk VIII	92	Italy		602	
	145			609, 610, 611	
	417		Mk IX	32, 33	Middle East
Mk VIII	17	Far East		43	
	20			72, 73	
	28			87	
	54 (Australia)			92, 93, 94	
	67			111	
	81			126	
	131, 132			154	
	136			185	
	152			208	
	155			225	
	352			229	
	528, 529 (Australia)			232	
	607			241, 242, 243	
	615			249	
Mk VIII	253	Balkan Air Force		253	
Mk IX	1	England		318	
	19			417	
	56			601	
	64, 65, 66		Mk IX	317	2nd TAF, European Continent
	74			401, 402, 403	
	118			411, 412	
	122			414	
	124			416	
	127			421	
	129, 130			441, 442, 443	
	132, 133, 134			485	
	164, 165		PR Mk X	541, 542	2nd TAF, European Continent
	222				
	302, 303				
	306		PR Mk XI	2	2nd TAF, European Continent
	308				
	310			4	
	312, 313			16	
	316, 317			26	
	328, 329			69	
	331, 332			140	
	340, 341			400	
	345			541, 542, 543, 544	
	349, 350			680, 681, 682, 683	
	401, 402, 403		Mk XVI	65	England
	411, 412			74	
	416			127	
	421			129	
	441, 442, 443				

Mark Number	Squadron Number	Area of Operations
	164, 165	
	234	
	317	
	322	
	331	
	340	
	345	
	349	
	401, 402, 403	
	411, 412	
	416	
	421	
	443	
	451	
	453	
	485	
	602, 603	
Mk XVI	567	England (AAC Squadrons)
	577	
	587	
	595	
	667	
	691	
	695	
Mk XVI	74	2nd TAF, European Continent
	322	
	340	
	345	
	349	
	401, 402, 403	
	411, 412	
	416	
	421	
	443	
	451	
	453	
	485	
Mk XVI	66	Italy
Mk XVI	5	Postwar Squadrons
	17	
	65, 66	
	129	
	165	
	595	
Mk XVI	501	Postwar Royal Auxiliary Air Force Squadrons
	601	
	604	
	607	
	609	
	612	
	614, 615	

APPENDIX G: ROYAL AIR FORCE GRIFFON-POWERED MARKS, SQUADRONS, AND AREA OF OPERATIONS

Mark Number	Squadron Number	Area of Operations
Mk XII	2	England/2nd TAF, European Continent
	11	
	19	
	26	
	41	
	91	
	129, 130	
	229	
	268	
	322	
	350	
	401, 402	
	411, 412	
	414	
	416	
	430	
	443	
	451	
	453	
	602	
	607	
	611	
	613	
	615	
Mk XIV	17	Far East
	20	
	28	
	132	
	152	
	155	
Mk XIV	2	Postwar Squadrons
	17	
	20	
	26	
	41	
	132	
	152	
	155	
	268	
	350	
	600	
	602, 603	
	612	
Mk XVIII	11	Far East
	28	
	60	
Mk XVIII	32	Far East

Mark Number	Squadron Number	Area of Operations
	208	
PR Mk XIX	2	Germany
PR Mk XIX	58	England
	541, 542	
	681	
PR Mk XIX	60	Far East
	81	
F.21	1	England
	41	
	73	
	91	
	122	
	600	
	602, 603	
	615	
F.22	73	England
	502	
	504	
	600	
	602, 603	
	607, 608	
	610, 611	
	613, 614, 615	
F.24	80	England

APPENDIX H: MERLIN-POWERED SPITFIRE MARK AND MANUFACTURER'S TYPE NUMBERS

Mark Number	Manufacturer's Type Number
Mk I	Type 300 (same as prototype)
Mk II	Type 329
Mk III	Type 334
Mk IV	Type 346
Mk V	Type 349
Mk VI	Type 350
Mk VII	Type 351
Mk VIII	Type 359
Mk IX	Type 361
PR Mk X	Type 362
PR Mk XI	Type 365
PR Mk XIII	Type 367
Mk XVI	Type 368

APPENDIX I: GRIFFON-POWERED SPITFIRE MARK AND MANUFACTURER'S TYPE NUMBERS

Mark Number	Manufacturer's Type
Mk XII	Type 366
Mk XIV	Type 379
Mk XVIII	Type 394
PR Mk XIX	Type 389/390
F.21	None assigned
F.22	None assigned
F.23	None assigned
F.24	None assigned

APPENDIX J: MAJOR VERSIONS OF THE SPITFIRE FIGHTER

Mark Number	Comment
Mk I	1,020 to 1,040-horsepower Merlin II or III engine; armed with four then eight .303 Browning machine guns
Mk II/IIA	1,175-horsepower Merlin XII engine; armed with eight .303 machine guns
Mk IIB	Merlin XII engine; armed with four .303 machine guns and two 20-mm Hispano cannons
Mk IIC	Merlin XII engine; first to carry bombs; was known early on as SRT (Sea Rescue Type) E (Spitfire)
Mk VA	1,470-horsepower Merlin 45 engine; same armament as Mk II/IIA
Mk VB	1,440-horsepower Merlin 45, 46, 50/50A engines; same armament as Mk IIB
Mk VC	1,440-horsepower Merlin 45, 46, 50/50A engines; featured the clipped "universal" armament wing developed from the canceled Mk III version with alternative armament of eight .303 machine guns and two 20-mm cannons, or four 20-mm cannons

Mark Number	Comment
Mk LF VB	1,440-horsepower Merlin 45M, 50M, and 55M engines; low-altitude version; thus, L prefix
Mk HF VI	1,415-horsepower Merlin 47 engine; armed with four .303 machine guns and two 20-mm cannons; high-altitude version; thus, H prefix
Mk F VII	1,565-horsepower Merlin 61 or 1,710-horsepower Merlin 64 engines; low- to medium-altitude version
Mk HF VII	1,250-horsepower Merlin 71 engine; high-altitude version
Mk F VIII	1,565-horsepower Merlin 61 or 1,710-horsepower Merlin 63/63A engines; low- to medium-altitude version
Mk LF VIII	1,720-horsepower Merlin 66 engine; low-altitude version
Mk HF VIII	1,710-horsepower Merlin 70 engine; high-altitude version
Mk IX	1,565-horsepower Merlin 61 or 1,650-horsepower Merlin 63 engines; low- to medium-altitude operations
Mk LF IX	1,580-horsepower Merlin 66 engine; low-altitude version
Mk HF IX	1,475-horsepower Merlin 70 engine; high-altitude version
Mk XII	1,735-horsepower Griffon III or IV engines; first version of the Spitfire to use the bigger, heavier, and more powerful Rolls-Royce Griffon engine
Mk XIV	2,050-horsepower Griffon 65 engine; armed with four .303 machine guns and two 20-mm cannons, or four 20-mm cannons

Mark Number	Comment
Mk XVI	1,720-horsepower Packard-built Merlin 266 engine; armed with four .303 machine guns and two 20-mm cannons
Mk XVIE	1,720-horsepower Merlin 66 (Packard-built Merlin 266) engine; armed with two .50 in machine guns and two 20 mm cannons
Mk FR XVIII	2,375-horsepower Griffon 67 engine; armed photographic reconnaissance aircraft; carried three cameras and two 20-mm cannons
F.21	2,050-horsepower Griffon 61 or 64 engines with five-bladed propellers; stronger wing; some powered by the 2,050-horsepower Griffon 85 engine with two three-bladed contra-rotating props
F.22	As above, but with bubble canopy, cut-down rear fuselage and increased tail surface areas
F.24	Same as F.22, but with increased fuel capacity; armed as F.22 with four 20-mm cannons

Appendix K: Spitfire and Seafire Powerplants

Rolls-Royce Merlin Types

Mark Number	Comment
Type C	990 horsepower; first to power the Type 300 Spitfire prototype (K5054)
Type F	1,045 horsepower; second to power the above—beginning in January 1937
Mk II	1,030 horsepower
Mk III	1,030 horsepower
Mk XII	1,150 horsepower; burned 100- rather than 87-octane fuel
Mk XX	1,440 horsepower; essentially the Merlin 45 without the low-altitude supercharging system

Mark Number	Comment
Mk 32	1,620 horsepower; used by Spitfire Mk XIII and Seafire Mk IIC
Mk 45	1,440 horsepower; mostly used by the Mk F VA, Mk F VB, and Mk F VC versions of the Spitfire and Seafire Mk IB
Mk 45M	1,440 horsepower; used by the low-altitude Spitfire Mk LF VB
Mk 46	1,100 horsepower; used by the Mk F VB and Mk F VC versions of the Spitfire
Mk 47	1,415 horsepower; powered the high-altitude Spitfire Mk HF VI
Mk 50	1,440 horsepower; produced for the Mk F VC variant
Mk 50A	Same as the Mk 50, but for high-altitude operations
Mk 50M	Same as above, but for low-altitude operations
Mk 55	1,100 horsepower; powered the Spitfire Mk F VC
Mk 55M	1,100 horsepower; used by the low-altitude Spitfire Mk F VB and Seafire Mk III
Mk 61	1,565 horsepower; used for the Mk VII, Mk VIII and Mk IX versions of the Spitfire
Mk 63	1,710 horsepower; used by the Spitfire Mk VIII and Mk IX
Mk 63A	1,710 horsepower; used for the high-altitude Mk HF Mk VIII
Mk 64	1,710 horsepower; used by the low- to medium-altitude Mk F VII
Mk 66	1,720 horsepower; powered the low-altitude F Mk VIII and F Mk IX fighters
Mk 266	1,720 horsepower; used to power the Spitfire Mk XVI series; built in U.S. by Packard Motor Company
Mk 70	1,475 horsepower; powered the high-altitude Mk HF VIII, and Mk HF IX fighters
Mk 71	1,665 horsepower; used for Spitfire Mk VII

Rolls-Royce Griffon Types

Mark Number	Comment
Mk IIB	1,500 horsepower; used by the prototype Mk XII
Mk III	1,735 horsepower; used by the production Spitfire Mk XIIs
Mk IV	1,735 horsepower; also used by Mk XIIs
Mk VI	1,850 horsepower; used by the Seafire Mk XV
Mk 61	2,050 horsepower; used by the Spitfire F 21, Seafire F Mk 46, and Seafire Mk 45 and Seafire FR Mk 46
Mk 65	2,050 horsepower; used by the Spitfire Mk XIV and Mk XVIII
Mk 66	2,050 horsepower; powered the Spitfire Mk XIV and Spitfire FR Mk XIX
Mk 67	2,340 horsepower; used by the Spitfire Mk XVIII
Mk 85	2,050 horsepower; powered the F.21, F.22 and F.24 versions of the Spitfire
Mk 87	2,375 horsepower; used by the Seafire Mk 47; contra-rotating three-bladed propellers
Mk 88	2,350 horsepower; also used by the Seafire Mk 47

Appendix L: Major Photographic Reconnaissance Versions of the Spitfire

Mark Number	Comment
PR Mk IV	Powered by Merlin 45 engine; carried a variety of cameras in varied combinations of 14-inch (F24), 20-inch (F8) and 36-inch (F52) focal lengths; carried an extra 66.5 gallons of fuel for a total of 218 gallons; formerly known as PR Mk V
PR Mk VI	Similar to PR Mk IV but modified to mount its F8 and F24 cameras obliquely
PR Mk X	Pressurized version of the Mk PR XI below; only 16 examples were built
PR Mk XI	Powered by the Merlin 61, 63/63A, and 70 engines; featured "universal" camera installation method for many different photo-recce mission profiles
PR Mk XIII	Armed low-altitude version of the PR Mk VI; capable of 422 miles per hour at 27,000 feet
PR Mk XIX	Powered by Griffon 66 engine; pressurized cockpit for very high-altitude photo-recce and mapping work; had a maximum range of 1,550 miles

Appendix M: Major Versions of the Seafire Fighter

Mark Number	Comment
Mk IB	1,470-horsepower Merlin 45 or 1,415-horsepower Merlin 46 engines; came with "B'" wing armament
Mk IIC	Same as above, but with "C'" wing armament
Mk LF IIC	Low-altitude version of above

Mark Number	Comment
Mk III	Also Mk IIIC with "C'" wing armament; powered by Merlin 55/55M engines; the low-altitude version (Mk LF IIIC) was powered by the Merlin 32; first mass-produced version of the Seafire
Mk XV	Powered by the Griffon VI engine; used "B," "C," and "E" wing armament configurations
Mk XVII	Powered by the Griffon VI engine; beefier landing gear and bubble canopy; same as photo-recce PR Mk XVIIs; also known as Mk 17
Mk 45	Powered by Griffon 61 with five-bladed propellers or Griffon 85 with six-bladed contra-props; like Spitfire F.21; nonfolding wings
Mk 46	Powered by Griffon 85 engine; similar to Mk 45
Mk 47	Powered by Griffon 87 or 88 engines; folding wings and contra-props; chin-type air inlet and increased fuel

Appendix N: Major Photographic Reconnaissance Versions of the Seafire

Mark Number	Comment
FR Mk 17	Like Mk XVII (or Mk 17), but with camera in place of aft fuel tank
FR Mk 46	Armed photo-recce version of Seafire F Mk 46; carried two F24 cameras (one vertical and one oblique) in aft fuselage
FR Mk 47	Same as above, but powered by the Griffon 87 or 88 engines; started life as Seafire F Mk 47 carrier-based fighters, but transformed to photo-recce aircraft after the war

BIBLIOGRAPHY

BOOKS

Andrews, C. F., and Morgan, E. B. *Supermarine Aircraft Since 1914*. Naval Institute Press, Annapolis, MD, 1981.

Dibbs, John, and Holmes, Tony. *Spitfire: Flying Legend*. Osprey, London, England, 1996.

Gunston, Bill. *Piston Aero Engines*. Patrick Stephens Limited, Sparkford, Nr Yeovil, Somerset, England, 1996.

Haining, Peter. *The Spitfire Log*. Souvenir Press Limited, London, England, 1985.

Jackson, Robert. *Spitfire: The Combat History*. Motorbooks International Publishers & Wholesalers, Osceola, WI, 1995.

Moyes, Philip J. R. *The Supermarine Spitfire Mk I & Mk II, Aircraft in Profile, Volume 2*. Doubleday & Company, Inc., Garden City, NY, 1969.

Nohara, Shigeru, and Ohsato, Hajime. *Aero Detail No. 8: Vickers-Supermarine Spitfire Mk I-V*. Dai Nippon Kaiga Co., Lmt., Tokyo, Japan, 1993.

Price, Dr. Alfred. *Spitfire at War*. Ian Allan, Ltd., Shepperton, England, 1974.

Spitfire at War: 2. Ian Allan, Ltd., Shepperton, England, 1985.

Spitfire: A Documentary History. Macdonald & Jane's, London, England, 1993.

Spitfire Mk I/II Aces: 1939–41. Osprey, London, England, 1993.

Late Marque Spitfire Aces: 1942-45. Osprey, London, England, 1996.

The Spitfire Story: Revised Second Edition. Arms and Armour Press, London, England, 1995.

Spitfire: Fighter Supreme. Arms and Armour Press, London, England, 1991.

Scutts, Jerry. *Spitfire in Action*. Squadron/Signal Publications, Inc., Carrollton, TX, 1980.

Thetford, Owen. *Aircraft of the Royal Air Force Since 1918*. Funk & Wagnalls, New York, NY, 1975.

Wagner, Ray. *American Combat Planes*. Doubleday & Company, Garden City, NY, 1982.

PERIODICALS

Dean, Jack. "Spitting Fire." *Airpower,* November, 1993. Sentry Books, Granada Hills, CA.

Green, Group Captain David J. "Spitfires Versus Hurricanes." *D.C.O. The Journal of the Spitfire Society*, Autumn, 1996.

Mizrahi, Joseph V. "The Fragile Few." *Wings*, February, 1989. Sentry Books, Granada Hills, CA.

"Weathering the Storm, Part 2." *Wings*, April, 1989. Sentry Books, Granada Hills, CA.

"Chaos in the Dark, Part 3." *Wings*, June, 1989. Sentry Books, Granada Hills, CA.

OTHER

Alexander, Peter. Letter dated 14 February 1997.

Allen, Flight Lieutenant Charles S. Letter dated 26 December 1996.

Benn, Squadron Leader William A. Letter dated 20 July 1997.

Cole, Colonel Alvin M. Letter dated 2 February 1997.

Green, Group Captain David J. Letter dated 23 January 1997.

Healey, Flight Lieutenant Donald K. Letter dated 4 March 1997.

Johnson, Air Vice Marshal Johnnie E. Letter dated 10 January 1997.

Mitchell, Dr. Gordon. *R. J. Mitchell: Schooldays to Spitfire*.

Morgan, Henry. Letter dated 12 December 1996.

Ross, Pilot Officer Tony N. Letter dated 8 June 1997.

Spenser, Michael. Letter dated 3 August 1997.

INDEX